IN THE PINES: LOST POEMS, 1972-1997

IN THE PINES:
LOST POEMS, 1972–1997

DAVID ST. JOHN

White Pine Press • Buffalo, New York

WHITE PINE PRESS
P.O. Box 236, Buffalo, New York 14201

Publication of this book was made possible, in part,
by grants from the National Endowment for the Arts
and the New York State Council on the Arts.

ACKNOWLEDGMENTS
American Literary Review: Disquiet Fortunes; Mirror.
The American Poetry Review: Seeing You.
Antaeus: Homage to Robert Johnson; Casino.
Black Warrior Review: Louis XVI's Library; Her Watch; The Hotel; London Flat;
Don't Talk To Me; The White Pony; Stairways and Fountains.
Boulevard: Quote Me Wrong Again & I'll Slit the Throat of Your Pet Iguana.
Carolina Quarterly: The Avenue of Limes; Tears Before Their Time.
Colorado Review: Aspects of Solange.
Columbia Review: Acadian Lane.
Field: Lost Magic.
The Georgia Review: 33.
The Gettysburg Review: My Grandfather's Cap.
Green Mountains Review: Broken Gauges.
Grove: A Winter Sermon.
Hayden's Ferry Review: Celestine in the Rain; A Message For Monique;
Lonely People in Lonely Places; A Fortunate Man.
Herman: Anna Temoigne.
Acknowledgments continue on page 176.

Book design: Elaine LaMattina
Printed and bound in the United States of America

1   3   5   7   9   10   8   6   4   2

Library of Congress Cataloging-in-Publication Data

St. John, David, 1949–
In the pines : lost poems, 1972-1997 / David St. John
p.   cm.
ISBN 1-877727-90-3 (alk. paper)
I. Title
PS3569.A4536152   1999
811'.54–dc21   98-19088
CIP

CONTENTS

For
Philip Levine & Charles Wright
&
In memory of
Larry Levis

THE DRAGON IN THE LAKE:
A PROLOGUE

The Dragon in the Lake

When Li Po was a child
He was scolded constantly by
His Father for...well,
Not telling lies exactly,
But for exaggerating
In beautiful but disturbing ways.
For example, if a butterfly
Landed in the plum tree outside
His window, Li Po would run
To his Father, calling out:
The double lips of Buddha
are praying in my tree!
If his mother
Dropped a handful of rice
Onto the packed dirt walkway
Of the garden, Li Po would look
Up at the clouds and wail:
The seeds of the universe
Have scattered across my life!
As you might imagine,
This habit annoyed his family;
So, one day, an uncle took
Li Po on a walk to cure him
Once and for all. When Li Po asked
Where they were going, his uncle
Pointed to the trail leading
Up the mountain, and said: *There,*
To see the Grandfather...
Now, Li Po had often heard
His family speak with reverence
Of the Grandfather, who had, Li Po

Knew, the strength of seven rivers
And the wisdom of the eleven ancient
Masters. Li Po was silent for
The first hour of the climb, but
When he saw a lizard, a familiar
Chameleon, leap from a branch
To a rock — turning the color of
Air! — he couldn't restrain himself:
Uncle! The blessings of the nether
World have passed before me!
The Uncle said: *Nonsense, Li Po;*
That's simply a chameleon. Invisibility
In lizards means nothing. Li Po
Was discouraged; if it were true
That invisible lizards meant nothing,
Then what could really matter
Anymore? Li Po and his uncle
Climbed up through the dusk
And on into the night. Suddenly
As they reached a bend in the trail,
A meteor shower painted the sky
And Li Po fell to his knees,
Proclaiming to the pines:
The Jewels of the Unforgiven
Have burst like blisters in the sky!
Oh the shimmering curtain of
The final veil...! His uncle
turned to him, saying: *Really now,*
Li Po. The chips of astral systems
Frequently visit our province;
Only a superstitious peasant makes
any real note of them. And Li Po
Began to wonder if his heart

Had again mislead him. In silence,
They walked on, climbing and climbing,
All through the night. Just
Before daybreak, Li Po
And his uncle came to the mouth
Of a small cave carved into the mountain.
Before it, there was a shrine,
And pine needles burning. The Grandfather
Stepped out to greet them...
Before either Li Po or his uncle
Could say a word, the old man pointed
Behind them; they turned
And saw, below in the distance,
The most beautiful lake, black as obsidian,
Glistening...and as they watched,
It began changing into the colors
Of a ripening peach — red flames, yellow
Streamers, blazing ripples...
It seemed to be shaking as it filled
With a light from below the earth,
A volcanic, seething light,
Answering the distant red planet
Pushing at the lip of the horizon. And
The Grandfather put his hand
On Li Po's shoulder,
Asking: *Do you know what that is,*
My son? But before Li Po could answer,
His uncle broke in, saying: *Just*
The sunrise on a summer's day...
The Grandfather looked at him,
Shaking his head, gazing
Out across the lake. He turned again
To Li Po, and said: *Only a man*

Without a spirit
Doesn't know the creature who stirs
In that water, burning each day
To rise into the world, to shed the silk
Waters that are the walls of
Its cocoon, to strip itself of its robe
Of scales! Only a man
Who has no future in the life
Of pure light doesn't sit each morning
Waiting to welcome the return
Of its Kingdom! With that the Grandfather
Stepped back into his cave. Li Po's
Uncle was white as birch ash. He said:
Li Po! Tell me! What is it that's there?!
And Li Po smiled, able at last
To say what he had known in his heart
All along. *There, Uncle,* Li Po said,
Lives my protector,

                    and my single song...

I.
THE ORANGE PIANO

California

"Who do you love?"

—Bo Diddley

My last night in California
She got up from the broken bed
Standing naked a moment
Before pulling on her boots only
Her boots with their stiletto toes
And lizard skins
Before pulling back the drapes
That covered the dusty window of
Our small room in the old
Stucco motel
        the window
A floor-to-ceiling checkerboard
Of opaque and clear panes
She looked out at the trucks passing
In the rain down the old section
Of Highway 99
        the rainbows
Of the spilled oil and neon mixing
On the rain-glazed asphalt
Of the parking lot
Maybe she was thinking of a moon
In the teeth of the Sierras
A moon setting in the mountains
Beyond her father's ranch
Where it would be
Clear above these storm clouds
Maybe of her husband just
Getting up to the late news and his

19

Shift at the mill
But as I reached by the bed to the low
Table where I'd thrown my watch
And before I could say *Come here*
Don't worry or any dozen stupid things
She began to rock slowly back on the heel
Of one boot snapping out the other
Like a whip kicking out one
By one the small
Square panes of the window
Each echoing richochet of glass louder
Than the drone of the trucks outside
And as the lights of the room
Next door flashed
On a moment their sudden glare
Hitting the windshields of the cars
Nosed up in front of every door
I grabbed her around the waist
And pulled her back onto the bed
Her fingernails slicing
The whole length of my cheek
Three long parallel lids
Of skin opening as the blood ran
Down onto my chest
                    I held her
Until the lights next door went off
As the sound of the rain the trucks
And the night grew
Now when I go back to California
I don't ask where she is
                        or why
I only know it wasn't the risk
That kept us meeting in motels

In the bars of Chinese restaurants
It was simply the desire to be
Desired
        the lie
The good lie told softly in the dark
Each night to keep believing
You're lucky
        more lucky than most
                that if
The world holds many dreams at least
One of them holds you

33

This is where I wanted to be
Today, on this hotel balcony, three
Stories above the boulevard
Watching the end of a summer's rain;
Here, on this plush wrought iron
Chaise, a bottle of "33"
In my hand — my favorite French beer —
Its label the same two tones of
Black-and-gold as the beat up Ford
I used to coax up the Coast
Highway, hell bent for San Francisco,
Fifteen years ago in California.
And just as nothing could
Save that '33
Ford, I know, this evening, looking
Down on a parade of students,
Models, pickpockets, cinéastes, cab
Drivers, terrorists, and single
Priest making their ways down St. Germain,
Nothing can save me from this
Birthday. Those sullen
Numerals stare out at me from these
Dead soldiers, each empty bottle
I've stood at attention
In a snaking line
Over the bare floor of the bedroom,
Then across the tiny Bokhara at my
Feet: with this last,
An even thirty-three! Christ, I
Know — don't tell me — it could be
Worse. I could be thirty-four...
And dead. Or home alone. Or even more
Wounded, and alive.

Thinking of Cuba

Sometimes when I am thinking
Of you, I think of Cuba; last night,
Dreaming of Havana, I dreamed of
You, not as a woman
Holding a long glinting spoon
Above her coffee
As the sugar spills in its slow
White waterfall into the steaming
Pitch below, but as a girl
I know —
Though she does not look at me,
Though she does not look
At the women in the plaza calling
For blood, more blood,
Though she pays no attention
To her mother starting to pack
Again, for New York. With
A single sweep
Of her foot, she levels the row
Of lead soldiers lined in the dirt
Like the firing squad we saw
Perform in its orchestral unison,
Once, though only the fragment
Of a newsclip, as you
Turned your face to the empty aisle.
When I think of you, I think
Of you walking those unraked fields
Of ash smoldering on the mountainside
Above the city I know
You would never return to, not even
Those times when I am thinking of you
Thinking of Cuba.

The Party's Over

So it's daylight on the street
Inside the air is frosted
By its stale parfait
Of smoke
         the fog
Off the river in lazy plumes
Hangs in the branches of
The plane tree
           you've fallen
Asleep on the wine-colored sofa
One leg hooked over its low
Worn arm
           blouse open
& tied loosely at the waist
So I empty the ashtrays gather
The glasses & hustle out
The last friend finally sober enough
To find her way home
             & all the time
She's humming that wicked song *Rien
De Rien Non je ne regrette....*
& before I know it
I'm humming it off & on & I don't
Know why all of a sudden I'm crying
I don't know why
I want to wake you I just want you
To explain
          yet I don't
Or I can't & I won't sleep now anyway
I'll just sit up talking to the one sparrow
Living up in the open attic eaves

The one sparrow who listens
                              so patiently
To every confession & the weather & who knows
Who only appears to be so ordinary
As she goes & comes & goes

Dancing

Home from school I found
As I found every day
The door to his room closed
& behind it
Faint music playing
On a tiny record player
The kind favored in the '50s
By teen-age girls
& I knew my grandfather was dancing
Leather bedroom slippers rasping
Over the wood floor
Arms hooked in the air
Around his imaginary partner
As he practiced the steps to those
Dances he loved
                labeling each 45
With a strip of white adhesive tape
On which he'd print in ballpoint
Cha-cha foxtrot samba tango waltz
& each Friday night he'd drive off
In his salmon-pink Studebaker
To the Elks Club or The Rainbow Ballroom
Where in his silk shirts & wildly
Patterned ties
              he'd take
A few turns out on the floor
His white hair slicked grandly back
His gold-rimmed spectacles so polished
They'd flash with the rhinestones
Of his partners' crude tiaras
& at 1 or 2 A.M.

I'd wake up as the front door closed
Listening as he felt his way
In the dark along
The narrow hallway leading to our rooms
Until at last he'd bump quietly
Into my door
                    move slightly
To his left & find his own room
& I'd hear the lights flick on
With a solid sigh of accomplishment
Then the complaint of leather
As he settled in his reclining chair —
At that late hour & after a night
On the town — to reread
Some favorite passage of Virgil
One afternoon
12 years later on his yearly visit
To my grandmother
                    he chatted
With a young woman I knew
As we sat on the patio overlooking
The beds of rose & iris but shaky
On his legs he asked if the young woman
Might help him on his walk
Along those paths that meandered through
The thick shrubs & summer foliage
& it was a successful walk it seemed
Because when they returned
My grandfather was beaming though
The young woman seemed
Confused as she
Poured the tea my grandmother
Had carried out onto the patio

& as we drove away
Waving to the two figures standing
A few paces apart in the shadow
Of the pepper tree
The young woman turned to me & said
He kissed me
     on one of the back paths
He kissed me on the mouth
I thought for a moment & then asked
If that was all
    she looked out
The car window & at the pines & oleanders
In the elegant yards we were passing
Then reached over
To place her long delicate hand over
My own hand where it rested
On the steering wheel
& smiling
    said very slowly *No*
He asked if some evening he could take me
Dancing

Lavender

There is no
Simple circumstance,
As when a boy hiding
In a closet
Beside the mannequin swoons
In the mist of
A grandmother's sachet.
The crooked
White sticks of the legs
And arms bent around
Him, as he imagines
He is older,
Standing in a wooded field,
The beads of lavender
Rolling
In the yellow
Grass. He buries his face
In the hollow of a woman's
Neck. She
Had been picking a bouquet.
It was a simple morning,
He was with her.
Not a solemn
Circumstance, like these
Mourners by the field
All ignoring
This couple as they walk
Over to the casket.
The woman tosses her
Flowers
In with the old girl

Stretched out like a doll
In an awkward and brittle
Repose. This pose
Of circumstances with its
White sticks
And lavender faces. That
Bouquet. That soft body
Of memory, buried
Like a child in the closet
Of an open field.

The Ash Tree

My grandmother led me out
Into her garden
Its two landscaped acres
Its layers of dark fronds rocking
Against streaks of waxy iridescence
Against the chromatic confusion of
Emeralds & jades
            I was five
The frail white bells of the wisteria
Lit the length of the terrace eaves
& the mums nodded their lavender heads
Beside the cool slate patio
& the long trailers of the climbing rose
Arced through the limbs of the oak
Like a sequence of scarlet lips
Parting on air
            at the end
Of one of the lawns — endless lawns
Sculpted to resemble huge
Hans Arp cut-outs floating horizontally
On the earth — stood the prize
Of my grandmother's garden
Her golden ash tree
I knew the name of our city meant
In Spanish "ash tree"
I knew that every spring the parks
& avenues blew yellow
With leaves
         & none
Was more brilliant nor more
Electric than this balloon of ash

Suspended in the summer light
As we walked back slowly towards
The house
            I looked up
At the south face of the living room
Its entire wall simply four huge
Panes tinted to shield
The lazy reader from the afternoon
Glare
            & from the lawn
One saw only the garden reflected
In the black glaze of smoked
Glass
            so before me as behind me
The leaves of the ash tree shook
Like the gloved hands of puppets
Like Aztec stars of the thinnest
Beaten gold
            it was
My grandmother would sometimes say
As if each March the dull bark
Broke quietly to release
Numberless angels
                    each aflame
& struggling to reach heaven before
Night fell before
They cooled & blew like ash away
The last spring of her life
She lay in a hospital bed wheeled
Before those windows
Where she could watch the garden
In its familiar bloom
                    & the ash leaves

Which were at that very moment as
She wrote to me
Beating in a rising April wind
The day she died
I thought of my final visit
When tired & weak & exhausted by
My own nervousness
She asked to be left alone to sleep
& I went out into the garden
As I walked across the lawn towards
The ash tree
            I thought I heard her
Calling & I turned to walk back
& saw only the black panes reflecting
As always
            the garden surrounding me
Reflecting too my own dim shape
Approaching
& suddenly I was sure I saw her
Chiseled face & silver hair flare
For an instant
            as perhaps
She raised herself up in the bed
To look out at me or the ash tree
Shaking behind me in the erratically
Gusting breeze
& as my eyes focused again
Upon the watery surface of the glass
I saw in that new angle
Nothing
        only those black
Windows filling with gold light
As if my grandmother's face appearing

As it had was the white spark
That set each blazing
As if each slender wing of ash had blown
Very quietly   very finally   to flame

Waltz

Coming out into the Lungotevere into a battering rain
that keeps attacking my windshield wipers
I see in a flash right in front of me
flowing with me into the traffic's
stream
a broad, white open page — maybe the double
middle page of today's
paper —
dancing gaily, desperately, caught up in the whirl
of a tire
a sort of last waltz before giving up
and surrendering itself into shapeless grey
pulp
that's then reduced to
nothing

Well here it is winter another
quick winter
so different from the black and pitiless
season so terribly long,
capable in other times of changing
the child into a boy the boy into
a man
that endless season of flames
of tears, which, when remembering it
thinking it over later, already inside of
spring
used to whisper Come on don't be afraid, if you loved
so much, well soon there'll be that much again, and more
you will love

Giorgio Bassini, translated from the Italian with Ilaria Caputi

Acadian Lane

Indigo against ocher, Atlantic
Blue abutting shore cliffs, bluffs, sand,
All the earth on Prince Edward Island
The red of dried blood, of weather-worn brick,
Of this rutted, twisting road leading down
Through the fishing village to the harbor
Where lobster boats rock, scarlet as lobster;
The bay's depth, smoked glass, reflecting the town.
A few dogs rustle in the heat of the noon;
The gulls, the bitterns lift, circling again.
A man is walking this Acadian
Lane, the fine red dust rising off his clothes;
He begins to sing a slow French tune —
La mer, la terre, le monde est seulement ces choses!

Stand by Me

When the solace of angels is named,
When the winds blister the academy,
When the first lesions of winter light
Scrawl their paths across the black sheet
Of the bed beneath the skylight,
When the algebras of my past repeat
Themselves drunkenly on into the night,
When the lemon peels twist
At the edge of the porcelain saucer,
When the door is closed behind me,
When the stilettos all stand at attention
The moment I step onto the subway,
When my future's looking dim,
Stand by me
                no matter
The declensions of light along the shore,
No matter the new color of my hair,
No matter the tattoo I've solicited
In a bar fight over nothing,
No matter the earrings on the dresser top,
No matter the motion of my body against yours
Breaking its own rainbow,
No matter what,
                stand by me;
If some innocent misanthropy unties me
From my new suede shoes,
If the many travellers within me all
Depart together, or if the one who's most
Rude & surly returns to you alone,
If every word I've lifted with such effort
Hangs in its residue of ash,

If there's still some consequence in this,
Stand by me;
          after the music
Rasps its way out of my chambered bones,
After the shuffle I'm famous for is reduced
To nothing but the white tracings
Of shoes on a sidewalk,
Numbered 1, 2, & 3...
After the legato which will leave me alone,
After the third day of prolonged applause,
After the newscasters impress upon me
The transitory nature of all earthly fame,
After my make-up begins to run like
Stigmata in the shadow of the klieg lights,
After the night before the night
You decide it really isn't
Worth it anymore,
          stand by me;
Because the antiphony of my conscience
Has become quite enough,
Because you remember me believing
Whatever it was that I believed,
Because it's getting late no matter which
Country, heart or clock we consult,
Because the outfield is moving in,
Because even the women on the Pirelli
Calendar are looking grim,
Because everyone has to forgive someone,
Because I miss you & it matters,
Because no one else wears the morning
Quite so well, stand by me, please;
Stand by me.

Providence

A little drunk he walked back slowly
Along the bank of one of the outer canals
Until he saw painted in a prim Dutch hand the sign
Of an ornate tankard   the sign of his hotel
& in the unlit hallway he took out his skeleton key
& opened the door to the wrong room
Urgency without remorse   light flooding the frame
& inside the room she stood engaged in a particularly
Secular form of self-discourse naked before
A full mirror   a few muffled apologies   he turned
& paused in the hallway wondering if this wasn't
An accident of fate   perhaps   the hand of providence
& then the door slammed firmly behind him

Nothing Personal

Certainly she wasted no words

Telling me things weren't working out
The way either of us had hoped & imagined
Of course she meant by that nothing
Personal   & I agreed
That there was nothing personal at stake

But I was amazed
As she leaned back in the first morning light
Filling the white - & - yellow breakfast room
How young she looked smoothing
The front of her silk blouse   & not at all

As wasted as she should have looked
After night after night of knocking back *Remy*
As she lost & lost more at blackjack & roulette

& as I laid her keys in an ashtray on the cherry bar
I felt her eyes cruise my body very slowly   even
Affectionately   & I knew I was   *someone*

On whom she'd wasted nothing but a little time

The Orange Piano

Plainly one's fears are never
Punishment enough

One must also live the life that proves
Each fear was justified & if
Like mine one's ambition for a life is failure
Then the work is hard in order to fail
So completely
No doubts remain in the eyes of one's friends
& therefore only a truly fine career

Is worth destroying

It was a day the color of an oboe
That is the voice
Of Noah's dove as it skims the newly
Bared reeds of the world
A voice that considers & remains
The echo of rain
Across the staunch oaks & maples
That rim this lake more emerald than
Her rings

& she has taken the early cable car

Up to the peak
To sketch & drink tea on the veranda
Of the cramped lounge filled with tan
Young women & skiing gear & used Leicas
& beside them the several angular boys
Without expressions

& over dinner of lake trout in lime spokes

Before I take up my nightly post
At the orange electric piano in the hotel's
Balcony bar & jazz
Up some standards for the drunks   here
As the chandelier of the dining room
Begins to sway in the heat
Of the huge fireplace where the waiters
Have stacked an especially precarious
& intricate rack of logs

The gold of their flames shaking the cut glass

Above us   I'll turn
& and take out the small diary embossed with a dove

& ask her about her day up
Where the view from any prospect she says
Is simply of these somber trails & random traces
Of those of us below *a world* still going

Its many predictable & ordinary ways

*   *   *

Orange is the color of the soul no
That's wrong orange is the color of the *eccentric*

Soul like that of the old man who rings
The Angelus bell at odd hours before sitting
Down on his unmade bed to play the violin
Until at his open window the gray & the brown

Squirrels arrive with their daily
Curiosity picking
Through the scattered rinds & peels he leaves
Along the sill to encourage his audience
To return   *to return*

Orange is the memory of smoke as it recalls

Flames rising off the bones
Which is only to say that lovers make
With their own figures a special
Figure for the imagination that pleases anyone
Whose loneliness each morning might seem

As resolute as mine as I walk with

My cup of coffee to the ballroom now empty
& dusty with disuse   where the only real piano
Stands in this "Old & Formerly Regal" hotel

Once known for its sulphur baths & lakes
Shaded in layers of green   *chartreuse emerald*
The unreal dead greens of envy & remorse

& as I sit at the old Beckstein grand

I try working over again
The closing passage of a concerto
I could never quite get right   that is never
With that proper shade of *orange* to it

Though at concerts no audience seemed ever
To notice   or to care

& one evening during my last season
& on my last tour   somewhere in the Midwest
I went on stage drunk   & as I was playing
That concerto I knew suddenly she was *there*
In the anonymous darkness of the night

& I felt her body calmly

Settling beside mine in the narrow spotlight
& slowly fine grains of sweat blew all around me
In the air   above the keys   & over my stiff cuffs

& as I finished the final passage at last
I looked up without thinking to where
I knew she'd be   sitting still as far from me
As ever in the deepest row *high* on the right side

Of the paradisal third balcony

*   *   *

Music is the voice of time

& therefore my father told me also the voice
Of God our greatest teacher & so

I was taught to play with reverence the solemn
& ecstatic notes measuring God's voice

As my father

Stood above my right shoulder himself
The greatest living teacher   critics agreed

II. LITTLE SAIGON

Departure

I had been dreaming of
An albino peacock
Strutting before me along
The sun-washed hallways
Of my school, the best
School in all of Saigon
The nuns had told my
Shy mother as they chatted
In French that first day.
A lovely girl, they cooed
To Mother as they stroked
The length of my braid.
That day, I looked out
The tall scrubbed windows
Of the office & saw it,
White as ash... & in my dream
The sky itself unfolded
As the peacock
Slowly turned to face me,
Just the two of us alone,
As it spread the fan
Of its tail I could see
Each elegant pale feather
Quietly catch flame...
Each feather burning like
The sails of the paper boats
We'd set adrift on the pond
Of the pavillion after
My father died, a Buddhist
Farewell to the departed.
In my dream, the peacock
Flamed steadily to ash,
Then blew silently away,

Floating along the sudden
Getsture of a summer's breeze,
& I started shaking & crying,
No... it was my mother
Shaking me, crying, as she
Whispered in my ear
So as not to wake my sister,
Ngoc Be, it's time! For weeks,
In secret, she'd met
With an old man who lived by
The tobacco shop, who knew
A Jack Pirate who'd take us
& the others on his boat, away
From this place, the new police
& the old police, the murders
Of our neighbors, Mother's
Friends... That night
She handed me the suitcase
She'd already packed for
My sister Mai Chi and me,
& picking up my sister with
One arm & her own bag
With the other, she led us out
Of our sullen, damp apartment
Into the maze of alleys & lanes
Of our district, towards
The waterfront & the boat we'd
Leave on forever, forever
Towards a sunrise
Spreading pale & milky as
The peacock's quivering tail
At the horizon, towards some
Place of promises as distant
As any new world.

Adrift

The man who took our money
Pushed my mother out onto the other
Boat. Ours was too crowded
Already, he said, just room
For the two girls now. He
Was grinning. When Mai Chi saw
His black tongue and missing
Teeth, she began to cry. Mother
Was waving to us from the boat
Beside ours, her boat filling
With more like us, scared
& hopeful. We stood so close
Against the metal rail
As she yelled over to us, *Ngoc Be,*
Mai Chi, don't be afraid....
And as the two boats
Moved out from the cove in
The deep black of that midnight,
Mai Chi and I crouched there by
The rail even as the waves crashed
Up around us. The Jack Pirate
Captain, paid off by
All of us, started drinking right
There, even before the lights
Of the patrol towers disappeared.
We hated him and he hated us.
Days and days. And by the twentieth
Morning the only food and water
Still left were his, locked
In the trunk at the back of the boat,
& we were still nowhere, nowhere.

Your sister, my mother had called
Out, *Take care of your sister...*
And when we both began to starve,
When Mai Chi's tongue swelled
Against her lips, her face
Peeling and cracked with a film
Of salt, I saw the Captain looking
At me, grinning at me. Even
At fourteen, I knew what
He wanted. *Give me water for my
Sister, and food,* I said. Then
He made me turn and face the waves,
My arms hooked over the metal rail.
Your sister's ugly like an animal,
He whispered, laughing, as he
Moved up against me from behind,
Pushing his hands and body up between
My legs as the waves below me
Waved to no one. For food, for water,
This is what happened to me for
Ten more nights, as we
Drifted, many of the men and women
Of our boat already collapsed along
Its filthy bottom, and dying,
Their children sprawled on top
Of them, none of them even lifting
Their heads to watch him as he'd
Push me against the side
Of the boat, as I faced the sea
And the stars splattered over
The blackness above and beneath me.
When the Australian fishing boat
Suddenly moved alongside us one

Morning, I was barely aware;
It was like a huge sunrise up close.
The fishermen carried us all
Onto their ship, giving us blankets,
Clean clothes, towels for the shower!
Then I saw two of the sailors from
The fishing boat lock the Jack Pirate's
Arms behind him, leading him off
As he yelled at them. I touched
Mai Chi on the top
Of her head. Then it was my turn
At last for the shower; for
The first time in weeks, I could
Wash the long streaks of dry blood
Off the inside of my thighs.

Little Saigon

At home in my French class
At school, the nuns made us skip
The chapter of our book called
La Vie Exotique de Hollywood!
But I read it anyway. A young
Parisian girl and her uncle
Go and visit all the movie stars.
Now, here I am in California
And anyone who passes by
On the freeway to Long Beach
Can see the sign pointing the way
To Little Saigon, where we live now,
Mai Chi and I, with my mother's
Cousin's family...even though
We wait each day for some news
Of our mother, that she
Has finally arrived at a processing
Camp, that someone reliable has
Seen her, or the last, most
Horrible news we will not believe...
Even now, after three years,
Because time means nothing
When I hope... I dream of her
Some nights, still adrift,
The only one still living, waving
To me in the blackness, saying
Ngoc Be, Mai Chi...I am coming...
Someday. But I know my mother's
Cousin is ashamed of us,
Perhaps because she still believes
It was I who stood over the Jack Pirate

Her smell of exotic flowers filling
The small room. *Ngoc Be,* she said,
Mai Chi...I want to take you back
With me to Paris; would you
Like that? Well, then
We started crying more, nodding
Yes, yes! & when I asked, *Why,*
Why now? Aunt Kahnh barely whispered
As she looked at us & said, *Ngoc Be,*
Mai Chi...your mother is dead.

The Marais

How strange it was to speak
In French again, though I suppose
The old lessons of the nuns
Have served me well. We live in an
Ancient house that I love, here,
In the district called the Marais.
On the ground floor,
Aunt Kahnh's husband Eugene
Has his business, like his father,
Selling elegant & elaborate picture
Frames, or making them especially
To order for museums & painters
All over the world! I love watching
The workers sculpt & chisel the wood,
Or lay out the fragile sheets
Of gilt. Sometimes, Eugene lets me
Have coffee with the painters,
Some very famous men & some no one
Has ever heard of — like
The handsome one who last week
Brought me some scraps of canvas
For the set of new paints
Aunt Kahnh has given me. I don't let
Anyone see my paintings though,
That is, anyone except
Mai Chi, of course. Eugene is good
To us, & even if Aunt Kahnh
Did not love him the way she does,
I would love him, though I do not believe
I have ever seen a man with so much
Silver hair, or a man who could drink
So much red wine with his dinner!

— That night, the night before
We left Little Saigon for good,
Aunt Kahnh told us that Mother did
Not suffer; Kahnh knew, she said,
Because a woman she trusted
Had been there, on the same boat,
When the storm came washing Mother
Overboard...her hand showing
Once above the waves, then
Nothing, that quickly she was gone...
That's what the woman told Aunt Kahnh.
Last week, one night I stayed
So long upstairs painting that Mai Chi
Was sent to bring me down for supper.
I had been working all day on my
New secret painting, but I showed it
To Mai Chi. It was of
Mother walking in old Saigon,
The beautiful streets of our childhood,
& beside her...the white peacock, its
Tail spread like a snowstorm along
The whole of the background horizon.
When she saw it, Mai Chi began to
Shake, then cry. *When I dream
Of Mother,* Mai Chi said, *I see her like
This, the peacock at her side,
Walking quietly at home...*
I held Mai Chi & we both stared at
The painting. *Yes,* I said, *Mother is
Telling us that she is finally safe...*
We stood there together saying nothing
Until Mai Chi looked up at me
At last &
Said slowly, *Ngoc Be! So are we...*

III
THE WHITE PONY

Louis XVI's Library

(at the Musée Carnavalet)

I think the finality of the circumstance allowed it:
His carriage packed entirely with books bound in green leather.
But Louis took with him not the library of a man about to die —
A man who'd look to a favorite poem for consolation,
Or to the volume that boasted pages still dark with Marie's
        powdered sweat —
Instead, he brought the classics, the world's and France's,
Those essential and timeless texts of a king
From which his library of state might, once again, be built.
Oh, foolish Louis; so much shrewder the lady who brought
To those desolate rooms her life's entire collection
        of perfume vials,
The good sense to understand nothing would be quite
So intolerable as the stench of months-old blood rising up
Beneath the punishing and daily dying sun.

My Days at the University

Each evening, after I've finished

My lectures in philosophy, I like to stroll
By the modest river that burns like a rope
Through the city,

Reciting those childhood verses
My nurse taught me at bedtime every night, silly
Rhymes about boys & girls, celestial bodies;

Songs about the plains of snow, the names of animals,
Minerals, & plants — & so on, so forth...

They were meant to amuse me, I know,
At those dreary moments just before sleep, yet
They were meant as lessons too, elemental lessons
I'd return to in the distant days my nurse
Knew would someday arrive —

These days, staining the windows with the dawn,

Flags of light unfurling from the peaks
As orioles touch & color the empty limbs
Of the last majestic sycamores, the few elms

Still lining the Imperial Avenue.
My favorite café is still there,
Its view of the Triumphal Arch. I go often,
Once or twice a week, for old times' sake,
& sit with a thin, folded newspaper;
My coffee steaming, I sing under my breath

The song about a zebra in the swaying palms,

Or that one about a boy going off alone to war
Carrying only a bucket of stars.

I know a bit more *why*, but when my nurse,
My poor tired nurse, sang that song's refrain:
Through the night's black veil

> *I lift my pail of light...*

I could think only of the magic of such purpose,
Such courage, & that boy —

Courage comes; courage goes...a little
Like those plagues erupting quietly along the bodies
Of these sick decaying elms, a solution
For which my lectures remain too local, banal,
Ethereal, bland — *what was that boy's name?*

So forgive me. Sisters, my friends...
How could I know then how it might all turn out?
Blame anyone you like, but when I stand

Alone at the oak lecturn
Reciting the brittle litany of ethics
Tattooed upon my tongue, the long list of failed
Gospels, or any cold law of the mind,

Remember — I want simply to be singing for you
The final verse of the boy who believed

In the sky's debris: stars, light, forgiveness, rain...

& leaves, history's, blown from the open heart.
A boy who left home & family to save his Republic,
The Republic of Cruelty & Nonsense —

A boy who carried only the stars' breath into battle;
Who succeeded, too well; who soon became any man
Returning home at evening by the spent river,
Lost within himself, within the simple

Insubordinate dark.

Oriental Brushstrokes in a French Château

I. Autumn Love Letter

I made a boat. A little boat of bread.

On it, I piled all the hair of yours
I'd ever saved, secretly, for all those years.
(Do you remember all those years?)

I set the boat out on the lake
Below your mother's house (she was away,
That day, at the races), then I released
The pigeons from their silver cage.
They noticed right away — *A nest floating
On their lunch!* So the pigeons

Will reward me, I know, flying off
To lead me to wherever you are this evening,
To lead me back into the present tense,
Your long living gaze, where

I'll be. Waiting.

II. Winter Evening

Evening, as always, fans
Toward the New Year. A slipper
Scrubs the polished cedar floor;
A girl thinking of snow
Settles in a chair beside the fire,
The pulsing fire (hearth lit, distracted).

The lake, by morning, a simple
Plate of crystals, scattered pearls...
How does a year move? Sideways,
Like a crab
Crossing the broken rocks, making its way
First into the shallows then to the deeper,
Blacker pools. I suppose her dream
Of a mimosa, those red fists bursting
In spring air, is simply every
Promise left to be kept. Just as these
Tides of sand moving beneath the twin sickles
Of the crab mean that it's time, truly time.
Again, *her...*

III. *Summer Garden*

It seems unlikely, the way
The plum blossoms hang
Upon the screen
Like dozens of ruby hummingbirds
Seen at a distance, this
Distance, my window
To the arbor in the garden, where
Someone sheathed in scarlet's walking,
Throwing her arms out loosely
To either side, now and then, pointing
To the old ornamental bridge
While she explains in detail to no one
The scattered petals of the climbing rose,
Blowing a little in the breeze,
Like these blossoms on the screen just now,
Shaking as you touch them, undressing,

Celestine in the Rain

We were lonely in those days. Celestine
Dressed all in gray, her distinctive soldier gray.

Each morning, the fumes of diesel hung in the air
While the doves smittered and fussed

On the ledges outside our windows. The whole fabric
Of the day rippled with a sense

Of the implausible, the necessary, the bizarre...
We thought we held a license as timeless as breath.

It was a life, a life, a *life* —
And nothing gave me such pleasure, then, as walking

Late at night along the Seine, with Celestine, in the rain.
There are some moments that never unfold, never,

Like starfish curled beneath the narrow lips of waves;
There are mouths that never close over the mouths

They still desire. So many movements in the wind, so many
Memories left out again, but none makes such a claim

As the memory of Celestine, walking in the rain...
There, beside the bed, a familiar bottle of wine. There,

On the imitation Louis XIV chair, the silk blouse.
Where were the late apologies, those self important pleas,

The casual arrogances of a man who knows he's right
About this *one* important thing? —

And the hand slowly tracing the white shoulder,
The shoulder resolving all of the delicate muscles along

The back? Where are your last regrets? There, there
Beyond the unshaded windowpane, with Celestine out walking

Alone; with Celestine, giving time the pulse of her own name...
There, out with Celestine in the evening rain.

Anna Temoigne

Oh Anna Anna Anna

Tell your husband to go away again
Tell him the banks in London are telephoning for him
All hours of the day and night
Tell him his portfolio is ablaze in Amsterdam
Tell him those numbered Swiss accounts have been fingered
By Interpol at last

Oh Anna Anna Anna I can't take it any more

These endless secret phone calls
Where you imitate the mewing of your several cats
Driving me wild with desire
Can't you be happy with the sailor's trunk of jewels
Can't you settle this once and for all

Oh Anna the tires on your Ferrari are going flat
It's been so long since you've come
To see me

Oh Anna Anna Anna please try a little harder

Then maybe the silver mermaid embossed
On your stationary will quit singing to me late at night

Oh Anna Anna Anna don't you miss my grilled radicchio

Don't you miss those Sunday Punchinello shows
Don't you miss those long memorable midnight baths
When we recited together every chapter

Of *Madame Bovary*
            Oh Anna Anna Anna

Now what will I do with this impossible love

A Message for Monique

Could he have been more blue
Waiting along the white-tiled platform
Of the subway as the day's news bled

Rolled so tightly in his damp hand

I don't think the sky above the Champs-de-Mars
Knows why you sit there watching the path
Looking up the street thinking

He'll be here soon certainly quite soon

After all why else would he
Have bothered to call or leave the folded
Messages in the iron grill of your door

This last a single sentence on blue paper

This urgency you've crumpled in your coat pocket
And whatever he wants really doesn't matter
As long as a part of it however small has

Something to do with you

Radio Eros

There is nothing
Sentimental about the body
Acting as a transmitter of — to? —
The wicked cosmos, & the message, if not clear,
Is brutally profound. So, lost heart, radio eros,
Distant evangelical flesh, despair only if you feel
Nothing at all, only when the signal fades
To the white of daily noise; otherwise,
Each new desire admits we're still alive,
If barely, & newly at risk again, thank our
Lucky falling stars.

Her Watch

It was Swiss, of course,
A design of platinum and gold he imagined
Would not be out of place on a snuffbox lately
Belonging to some modern Marie Antoinette;

And though half-obscured by the long sleeve
Of her peach-colored blouse,
The watch still gave off a kind of glow,
And he thought he could hear not the comic ticking

One associates with seconds passing in those scenes
From old movies but, instead, the faintest humming
Of crystal as the white tiers and stairways of
Quartz were touched by the coarse pulse
Of her own blood,
Each vulgar spasm of flesh above the vein

So unlike this cool mirror of beaten metals,
And perhaps not nearly so precious
As he'd thought at first — at least, not to her,
For whom the engraved inscription still pressed
Like a fallen tombstone along the bone of her wrist;

Though she continued like a proper slave
To flash the elegant manacle, as if it still linked her
To some ancient and extravagant ritual, or some still
Immaculate faith in time.

The Hotel

A friend had once in passing
Mentioned this hotel, in a truly tedious letter
Meant only to inspire my jealousy
For her exceptional room and its polished
Stone veranda, where she'd sit out at twilight
Each evening, listening to the first sobs
Of the nightingales. So, I
Suppose, I decided to stay there simply
Out of some sentimental impulse, some old
Allegiance to that long-dead friendship.

I stood at the desk, describing in detail
The room I wanted, and the clerk
Began nodding slowly as if he could recall
Every face that had ever
Entered or left its carved oak doorway.
As I filled the register with my elaborate
Scrawl, meant to intimidate publishers
And lawyers, he turned with a melodramatic flourish
To pull the brass key from its nest
In the dark grid of pigeonholes and forgotten mail.

That evening, after the sun had set
And the nightingales had sent the stars along
Their mechanical course, I came downstairs
To find the day's newspapers,
Or a brandy, or some excuse to ease my restlessness.

Then I heard from the music room
The opening of my favorite Chopin nocturne, played
Perhaps a bit unsteadily at first, but then

The Avenue of Limes

She was whispering to the leaves
As the first nails of shade crossed the pathway, slowly
Latticing the bright parched yellow of the earth
With their violet limbs, mirroring the faint
Trembling of the arbor above. Swallows
Broke here and there out of the branches,
Arcing into the growing twilight gold, rising and falling
Like the black capes of angels fired
By deeper coals, by time. It gave a sense of ending
To their walk, even more so as he let his hand
Drop from her arm. As they walked
The long cool avenue of limes toward the ruins
At the path's end — the old manor house — a slow
Silence began to choke her. She knew soon,
In the meadow spread before the fallen stones and ashen beams,
He'd turn to announce their future. And it would
Always be this way, she believed...
The smell of ash, the cold touch of granite washed by the rain,
His promise of the days rebuilt with children.
Still, it was the taste of him she could not forgive again,
Like the paring of a lime peel she'd
Torn slowly across her teeth. Bitter. Wild as spite.

Don't Talk to Me; Touch Me

The hummingbirds stitched
The palm fronds, and the sun went down, and down...
He jammed a rum bottle
Between the cushions of the sofa, opening a window
So he could listen to the salsa band
At the Armory, lazily tuning up before the evening
Dance for the island tourists.
Outside, his motorcycle glistened like a black mantis
As he began slowly pulling on the shiny
Flowered shirt and striped pants that women loved
To touch underneath the arc-rainbow
Of lights, while he'd carefully choose the one
Who'd certainly have money or jewelry back at her room —
A small price to pay for a man with a waist
Like a cat. And besides,
In that part of the world, well, wasn't that sort of thing
To be expected, those nights
A leopard light still hung upon the walls?

Tears Before Their Time

Late feathers of cloud broke
Beyond the first glint of circumstance, and she stood
At the gate, pulling his last letter
From its wooden box — the letter's intentions
Stamped with palms in several garish colors,
Showing off those distances still
At stake between them, between her fingers tearing
The lip of the envelope and his hand still smeared
With violet ink reaching
For the iceless rum on the card table where he sat,
More than a world away,
Solitude spread out before him, its few royal faces
Obscured by the simple fan of night. No tears,
She'll remember later in her diary, except
Those along the faint fur of the peach she'd wished
To pick outside her window, the one shaped imperfectly
As the globe she'd spin each evening
In her father's library, looking for those delicate black lines
That might band the dark distance to his hands.

Lonely People in Lonely Places

Clarisse had been polishing the plates
Even though no one was expected for dinner;
Somehow, it made her feel a bit more alive
As she listened to the dogs
Barking along the lane, marking the progress
Of the postman toward her door. He'd
Certainly have something for her today, perhaps
The glass chimes she'd ordered from Boston,
Or the pewter ladle her sister had promised
After their mother's death. Maybe there
Would be her box of narcissus bulbs. Soon,
She'd be planting
& praying to all the goddesses of the moon
For another spectacular season, her usual
Triumphant garden — one that made
The strolling couples pause & lean together
For a moment, their breaths mingling in the brisk
Spring air as they regarded that precise chaos
Of blown color she'd used
To surround her cottage. She loved to watch
As they stood at her white gate, pointing & exclaiming
At the layers of fern & crocus, wild heather
& rose, holding each other a little
Closer before they turned, disappearing up the lane
To the village. Singularly content, & pair by pair.

The White Pony

I'd never really given it much thought —
As an *idea*, I mean — the sense of homelessness that
        Seems to have been the very melody
Of my life. Orphanhood should, I think, be something
      Left to English novels. Yet, when my
Father took my mother out sailing late one afternoon
        Into some quite extinguishing silence,
All I was left with at fourteen years old
      Was a Gladstone bag of scarred white leather,
        And the photo of a white pony
In full gallop across the tall reddening grass of my
      Grandfather's fields. Slouched on the back
Of that pony, my cousin — still a girl herself —
        Only eleven, maybe twelve... And
Though I'd never given it much thought,
      As an idea of harmony, I mean, that night as she
        Walked into Celestine's
Dressed in black pants, black riding boots, barely
      Wrapped in a white leather jacket over, it appeared,
        Really nothing at all...all of my long
Homelessness arrived at once, an utter loneliness
      That had followed me like the blank wake
        Of a crippled sailboat,
Off course, off the charts, off the very face of the earth —
      Its wake spreading like a young girl's hair,
Like the mane of a white pony galloping
        Through the red Virginia fields. And if
Love is this world being torn apart by possibility,
      Then this was love; if love is a kind of homecoming
        Of the senses, then this was love;
        And if love is

A total and incapacitating sexual obsession, then
        This was most certainly love...

                    *   *   *

After the party, I walked her back
        To the Marais, to that room above the storefront
Nikolai'd slowly turned into a simple studio
                For ballet, giving her the small room upstairs
For almost nothing. Sometimes, Bella cooked for three,
        And they were, she said, like parents, always
Looking after her, caring for her the way
                Her true parents never could, not even
        If they'd once thought of it, simply stopping by
At Grandfather's now and then to leave some presents,
        To stroke her hair, to say
Goodbye on their way to the Orient, London, San Francisco;
        Always some new destination where they'd
Prefer to spend their time. And in
                The small bar we stopped in, on the way home
To Nikolai's, a sweaty dive filled with smoke
        And other people's laughter, she told stories
In an accent so American – so like my mother's
                And so like her own mother's –
        It made me homesick for those summers
At Grandfather's, where, after various aunts had grown
        Weary of my silence, I would arrive carrying
                My beat up white Gladstone,
The bag filled with only a few clothes, and my single
                Photo – its ghostly pony snorting just outside
                The open window, the same cousin
Looking up so casually from her redwood chaise...
                The house of my Grandfather, house of our

Mother's house of the red fields blowing...
                    From my room on the second floor
        I could watch the pony grazing lazily
By the stream that edged the field, its boundary marked
            By a thick line of poplars,
And each day I'd stand at the window as the sun just
        Broke through the net of leaves,
Waiting for her to come out riding; it was silly,
            I know that. Yet this was
What I lived for, truly, everyday...every night.

                    *   *   *

One summer, I arrived to find her gone —
        Off to Richmond, a camp for young ballet dancers.
I was so bored I began to spend my afternoons
            Reading to Grandfather my favorite passages
From Sartre, just to hear him yell with disgust,
        Just so we'd have something to argue about,
To pass the time over in those days before
            I'd leave for good, leaving behind everything—
Wanting to take with me nothing of my
        Other lives, the transience of those homes
                In the homes of my numb relatives...
I wanted only to take with me the memory of
        Grandfather's cavernous voice
            As he screamed at me that Sartre was
A *goddam* bloody fool — And the photo,
        That photo of her in the burnt summer fields. Then,
One evening, I decided I would live, as a romantic
                Seventeen year old decides,
As they said in the movies, "abroad"; I loved
        The way that sounded. The word carried with it such

Grandeur, such an indeterminate sense of mystery,
              That I knew *this* was the world
         Where I would live—not in a city, not in any place
So *particular,* but simply
              In that place of mystery — vague, aloof, *abroad...*
When she wrote to me (the postmark, Richmond; the scent
              Of the envelope, "White Shoulders"), she said
Simply, "You've become our mothers, leaving us;
                         Don't write to me again." For
Years I did, though she never answered, even if,
              Admittedly, my addresses changed so often
Even Grandfather's lawyers grew confused. And yet,
         That summer I wanted nothing I could imagine —
I wanted only to find somewhere in the world
                    Whatever was still unquietly
         Waiting to be mine. One evening, as thunderheads
Rolled in from the west, Grandfather pointed
              To the faint greenish tint riding the soft lip
Of the oncoming storm. Without a word,
         We began closing the heavy shutters and the storm doors.
Our usual precaution, a drill we had down so well
              That soon we were back inside, Grandfather
Twirling the dial of his old cabinet radio,
         Trying to pick up anything but the usual static.
I went upstairs to my room, sitting with the lights
              Out, waiting for the storm
         Rippling, unfolding over the hills, moving
Now in double time toward the long valley
              We lived in; split forks of lightning splayed
         Out of the black mass of the nearing clouds,
Striking here and there in the distance. Then,
              All at once, the lightning was firing
                    Into the poplars just beyond

The stream. The white pony moved quite suddenly
        Away from the trees, trotting
                In large circles, then driving into a gallop
Back and forth across the whipping grass —
        I yelled downstairs to Grandfather, but
The storm was on us. I could hear the air begin to crackle
              As a huge strike lit up my room,
All of the circuits in the house blowing;
         And in that blackness, the lightning colored everything
A translucent green...I looked out to where
           The white pony stood turning
In tight circles, shivering. All at once, she broke from
        Beneath my window towards the stream,
                Leaping suddenly as if
She were clearing an imaginary fence or hedge, lifting
        All four hooves off the ground,
           Her mane trailing like a scarf delicately
Behind her...and at the apex of her leap, a single
        Finger of lightning touched
              Her forehead, and she stiffened —
Her head still lifted high — then she fell,
        Briefly, standing up slowly again, trembling
         Like a snow-laden willow
Before collapsing at last for good. I ran down stairs,
        To the room where Grandfather sat...knocked back
         In his chair, his eyes still wide,
His lashes slightly ashen — two fingers seared black
        Where the tide of electricity had passed
             Through the steel knob of the radio —
        Amid the static, some old swing tune
Arose out of nowhere. I kicked over the charred cabinet...
                 I remember only
Walking outside, into the shifting pages of the rain,

Across the scarred fields, to the body
Of the white pony, still twitching beneath impulses
             Of current...I held
      Grandfather's rifle to the small rounded bump
Below the uplifted ear...

                              That first evening,
In the bar with her, I couldn't find the way to tell this;
      Then, one night, over dinner with Nikolai and Bella,
After hours of vodka and Ukrainian folk songs...

                        I knew, at last, I could begin.
Nikolai raised his glass, toasting the white pony,
      Or anyone, he said, who'd simply lost a home...
The next morning, hungover, I walked along the quiet Seine
             From my place on Cardinale Lemoine,
Walking slowly, knowing that only I wanted to see her,
      To watch her taking class with Nikolai;
I stood across the street, watching her at the barre
             Mirrored and erect, head slowly lifted
To Nikolai's instructions, his mouth moving silently
      Beyond the latticed storefront window.
In her white leotard, she looked like a ghost reflected
      Upon the water; her hair, almost silver
In the morning light, tied tightly back with a green ribbon,
             A long ponytail falling along
      Her back, onto her bare shoulders. I stood there
For an hour, maybe more, utterly at peace, barely noticing
      As rain lightly started to fall. When, finally,
She'd finished for the day, climbing the narrow stairs
             To her room, I walked across
The street to the studio, standing before its perfect wall
      Of mirrors. Nikolai'd wrapped a thin blue towel
Around his neck; he sat at a small table,
             Staring off into the air at nothing. When

He heard my step, he rose, turning to me the way Grandfather
     Slowly turned, embracing me, saying my name
Over and over, as if I were the last prodigal come home —
      "She's upstairs." And I said, "I know...."
Then that night, she and I in bed together, rain slipping
     Over the city, sketching its solitude on the sky, its
Useless addresses, its irrelevant pasts —
      That night, together, all the way, slowly, so
Slowly together, we rode together, slowly,
        All the way, all the way home...

Stairways and Fountains

I. In the Valley

(Blois)

More than the scent of flowers
It was the soft fragrance
Of chocolate in the air, the Poulain
Factory nearby smoking and huffing
Like a child's dream of heaven on earth.
And the towers of all the châteaux
Rose along the river, both sides
Of the valley dotted
And pocked by slate tile roofs, blue
As wounds. The other scent
That clung to the stones was the scent
Of blood, centuries old, as voices
Everywhere in the night named
Their king, their Henry, their assassin...
And the Medici women sighed
In the ornate galleries, disappointed again
By the king's persistent failure of
Imagination. Blood, the real, that's all
That he knew; the trusted blade
Running along the bone of the lower
Rib. So much for God's messenger;
So much for his blessing of
Eternal peace. And sitting on the spiral
Of the external stone stairway...
A boy is drawing the little chapel
Across the courtyard, its modest steeple
Hardly to be noticed at all. It was
There, he knew, that they'd worshipped —

Those who continued in man's long
Tradition of man's never-ending fall...

II. 1527, The Fall of Rome

Likewise their fortunes, and the fall;
And the city bled. The weak wept, the weak fled.
Everyone else was already dead...
The aqueducts, blocked by stones; the fountains,
Dry for the first time in years. Those stairways
Gleaming in the sunlight rose still to heaven,
Though the veins in their marble burst,
And the steps slickened
With the red of the season's end, little leaves
Falling and flowing into the fountains —
The dry fountains and the red stairways. The legends
Of languid lives, lost lives, the spigots gone hollow,
And bodies in their endless blank ascension...
Likewise, their fortunes, and their fall.
This was the music of demise, a melody played
First for others, then sung again beneath
One's own shattered eaves. If what's truly
Monumental about these dead
Exists so grandly in the simplest fragments,
Then it's time's revision that's worn each down
Into this state of grace. Tonight,
Forget it all. The only time
That matters is this time, this present we know,
Which leaves us simply these few urgent fountains,
These sexual stairways, and hardly any
Time, hardly any time at all.

IV.
THE OLIVE GROVE

Lunch

Even the morning dreams of it

Bent over those torn envelopes or steaming
Papers those Cubist towers
Of paper clips and pink erasers

We think we understand so much but nobody
Ever mentions the secrets of lunch

We plan to meet in some café
As the sunlight pours off the buildings
Onto the striped canopies the umbrellas above
The white tables

As usual I'll be late
Stopping on the way to look at books or scarves
Wondering how you'll tell me
Finally to go screw myself once and for all

The secretaries leaving their martinis
The executives phoning in from God-knows-where

I even knew a man who ate lunch
In typewriter stores driving all the clerks mad
Leaving cigarettes burning on the display desks
Rye seeds in the immaculately polished keys
Even notes in the carriage

So here we are again bent over
Those inscribed tablets those endless commandments
Of the menu

Where the choice of wine is blood
James Joyce once said or clear electricity

From the Notebook

Cathedrals of rock, blue
Zones, pools and fiddler crabs.
A white sea snail
Sleeps suspended in the light.
The signature of cypress
Against the sky. In these dawn
Tidepools, these
Intimate worlds left standing,
Minute horses and bandit worms
Stretch through threads of vine.
The red ferns, branches of my eye;
The keys of lichen and trumpets of
Coral the wild lamps
Of that other, perpetual night.
Once, you asked, *Why do sand*
Dollars die with their leaves
Outstretched,
Like the star of a man's body?
Clocks of five hands and no numbers,
Fit for the pocket but lost at sea.

Seeing You

As if you were in Switzerland, again,
The water soothing the sunsets,
The mad. Landscapes of memory, release. Your
Old painting of Dante asleep,
Hanging in that cold, blue room. This exile
Of tranquility.
A new bed, the strict mountains above you—
The doctors' soliloquies, no pale wine.

Do you remember the train? Those wings
Battering the windows, you said,
Of the compartment, like the two great wastes
Of your life: a father *dying, a time!* Those boys
Whistling so sexually on the platform
As the windows darkened all along the rails.

Who cares? Even the swallows will leave,
Rippling off the wires like black and white waves.

A new truce in the storm. The day burnt
Red. As even the orchids in the greenhouse
Step up, licking at the yellow panes. The moon
Horning in on the dusk, hanging above the bay.

So, once in a while the seasons polka,
The sun unrolls like a road...

Once, we filled your loft with feathers,
Tore the icicles off the pipes. We watched
Morning pull up like a silly gondola
Its song of tar and dollars, trucks. Wagons of

Salt. Bells up
The street. The black doors like widows
Closed on the churches. The earth's piano! That city
Knew the tune to use, which zones of sale, which
Loose news to drop.

You say, forget that. You say, Pasternak
Had a face like a lovely horse. I cut his cheek
With my nails. A face like November.

We turn back up the path, to the rooms and baths,
The white glare of buildings. Well, you say,
So that's the way it is. Your scarf
Falls onto the grass. The precise yellow grass.
When I go, again, I repeat —
My life holds down a few papers, a few sheets, not
Much, that's all...

A Winter Sermon

After Blas de Otero

This is the passage
We describe
As that of one land
To another,
Of ignorance to faith —
The way light passes
Through smoke,
Through the islands
Of glass, onto a floor.

Or, through
The space of His arms
Into our arms, all of us
Praising and rising
In the light.

A hand in this house,
A breath. A will
Sifting
Down the bones of a child:

This passage of hunger
Into dust.

It's your hand, Lord,
Stiff claw and palsied glove,
Your hand making the child
Kneel as he is blessed —

And in Your name, named!

If You are the Lord, then we
Are equally men,
You
With Your two hands
Like bowls of hunger,
That
Even now You'd push in front of us.

Homage to Robert Johnson

> *There's a hellhound*
> *on my trail*

Sometimes the moon
Rides these trees like a red feather
Walking its milk light through the branches
Onto these long beds of pine dust
And yellow needles

I sit on the porch scraping my boots
Over the rough boards

I used to sleep with a woman who swore
Each morning the anger rose in my bones like dew
That in my dreams I beat her
Like a coat
So I pushed my thumbs beneath her cheekbones
Until she knew why all along this delta

The oil fires flared

Like the tracks kicked-up behind the devil's
New shoes
She sleeps with the child now I don't mind
I just sit up late on this porch

Watching that boy drive
Back and forth in his silver Terraplane
The boy with a face like a woman's the voice
Of a hurt cat
Like the tine of a steel fork striking glass

I think I'll go to the Amarillo
I know a hotel where the rooms open like memory

Onto fecund nights
Onto rains still blue or blouses empty
The vein's filament still lit in the crook of my
Elbow the spoon burned to a bruise

The asphalt roads quiver in the heat
Salvation setting like a moon in its last black
Spiraling range of sky.

Welcome

Never is anyone else
At home. In the village they
Will tell you
I'm religious, or dull.
Distracted by the smallest, first
Movement of the dust
Rising in the wash of sunlight
Through the trees. My wine goes
Flat and sour;
My cheese wears the bad green
And spreckled complexion of the leper
In his hood of wax. Even
Those goats my father left to me
Are dry as gloves. The dog will lick
Your shoes, which is nice
Except he will not stop. The fire
Is ash. There is no
More wood and no forest I would cut
To burn. Yet, without you, I would let
The clothes mold right off
My body. I would let the birds walk away
From their eaves, into that sky
Heaving its ice. Nothing else matters.
Without you, things grow worse
Than they seem. Please,
Now that you are here, come in.

Heartbeat

My father's eyes fix again
On nothing.
My mother cries,
And holds his mad wrists
Against her forehead
For the seventh day.
Heartbeat: 212.

In the riverbed,
A nervous, blood-haired roan
Sniffs the darkness
Curled at the wind's edge.
And runs;
And can't stop.

Nostrils blaring.
Mad hooves clattering on the shale.

The Missionary

Began like the other boys —
in quiet hours, picking flies
off dogshit

with a Crossman air rifle.

Saw, one night,
his soul leak out of his body
like air from a slashed tire —
watched it soar and ramble
across the fat, summer
stars.

Found God in the shell
of a hermit crab, and gave it to his kid
brother.

Walked the Sierras
naked in winter, digging his fingernails
into his chest; and disappeared.
Mexico?

Brazil? Just the rumors —
a wild Christ & lost tribes.

His friends dreamed of loaves,
of smoke rising in cold
pueblos. And of a man on their
porches, singing a
Spanish hymn.

A man grinning like a bear.

A bottle of fine German beer in
his hand, a machete. A tiny
silver crucifix,

dangling from his ear.

An Afternoon:
The Hotel at Portage-La-Prairie

Lerida sighs,
shows her veins of scab,
and tells how the moon winked
and went black;
how a garden of ice bloomed
in her skull — how she blew it
and woke up alive.

She drags her fingers
across the raw, unvarnished
headboard; then lifts her hair
to show the birthmark
where the Lord touched her: a red star
blazing, just below the ear.

And says yes, she'll
sleep now.

Downstairs,
I watch the prairie winds blow
along the empty street, sip coffee,
sketch her name on the table
with a burnt match, and take out
the note that brought me. No words.
A piece of torn wrapping paper —

a child's painting:
a meadow of pale grass, some pines.
A stick-girl climbing the sky; in one corner,
a black coin, a moon.

Casino

There is no casino like the heart's.

Those lovers and gamblers walk the park,
Through oaks or pines, along the lawns of felt
Where some croupier rakes his perfect stick.
She's lost her touch. He owes an uptown shark.

There is no casino like the heart's.

V.
BROKEN GAUGES

Broken Gauges

Some moments
Hold their grace in ways
That seem more
Than momentary though the solitary
Believe this to be true
More often than it really is
Up late & talking
With old friends I haven't
Seen in years
I know fewer of those moments
Still penetrate
The past   & if those friends
As they sometimes do
In all sincerity & confusion ask
How am I these days
I simply say: *Think of me as*
A truck with broken
Gauges driven a few times
To hell-&-back
By a man a lot like me...

* * *

I was nineteen
& it was midnight & two hours
Outside of Winnemucca
Nevada when I finally hitched a ride
With a drunken cowboy
In a '62 Ford pick-up with four spools
Of steel cable & part
Of a transmission in the back

119

He'd weave back
      & forth across the road singing
           Along with the radio
I didn't mind at least I was moving
           At least I wasn't
Back there by the side of the highway
           But pretty soon
With the first glimmer of lights
           In the distance I could
See his tongue starting to work
           Inside his mouth & as
The bar sign came clearer I knew
           There was no way
He'd pass it by without a little
           Something for the road
Then he hit the brakes & we slid
           Half-way across the gravel
Lot before we stopped almost exactly
           At the door & once inside
We hunched down at the bar & started
           Talking like old friends
I bought him a shot of whiskey
           To go with his beer
& then another & then one more & then
           Finally his head just fell
Forward onto his crossed arms & sort of
           Died there   well   *Goodnight*
Cowboy   I lifted the keys
           Out of his jacket & winked
At the bartender saying *I'll go out*
           & get him a blanket from
The truck   & outside I stepped casually
           Up into the cab

Found the right key & hit the ignition
             & as the engine turned over
I looked up to see the bartender's face
             Rise up above the limp
Red curtains in the window so I waved
             I knew that cowboy couldn't
Move a muscle   I put my foot down
             On the accelerator
All the way to the floor & with the gravel
             Of the parking lot spraying
Out behind my tires I fish-tailed out
             Onto the empty highway
Wondering how long I had before
             The bartender phoned
The police & then how long after
             But the night was perfect
Cool & black with lots of stars just
             Clattering around up in the sky
I was going fast but
             When I looked down to scan
The beat up metal dashboard I saw
             The needles of every gauge
Lay motionless   absolutely still
             Speedometer   tach   oil pressure
All glowing there like dead clocks
             With single broken arms
Oh Christ   I thought   I've stolen
             A truck with broken gauges
So I pressed my foot down harder
             On the petal until I must
Have hit just over 100 as the first
             Little wisps of steam
Started working their fingers out

Around the edges of the hood
Then with one enormous white belch
Of astonishment
The radiator finally exploded
Boiling water flecked
With rust pouring up over the windshield
I just held my foot to the floor
The smell of scorching oil filling
The truck's cab then
Like rifle shots & arms snapping
The rods threw & the engine
Began to pay out its metal treasures
All along the highway
Accompanying itself with a high whine
Like steel fingernails
Scraping the eternal black of sky
& I edged the truck
Closer to the roadside as it began
To slow   a rolling
Kaleidoscope of nuts & bolts
Then I turned down a dirt farm road
The truck coasting now   & aimed
Its nose off the road
& out into the desert where at last
Its wheels settled in a long
Plush bed of sand & I got out just as
The engine died in its retching
Staccato steel-warping collapse & walked
A circle around the old truck
Patting each fender & the twisted side mirror
Goodbye   then I grabbed my rucksack
& set off walking into the desert
Until I came to the railroad tracks

Where I began to follow the rails due west
      Far enough from the highway
I hoped that neither police nor vigilantes
      Could find me & with the faint
Chords of dawn striking behind me to the east
      Ahead I could see on the horizon
The first soft sparks that were the lights
      Of awakening Winnemucca

          *   *   *

      Some say twenty years
Is almost forever & some say it's
      Nothing in a man's life
In all the separate individual lives
      We lead in those years
& I know that I believed in
      Every one of those lives
Or almost every one   at least
      I believed every lie I told
I told for some good reason even though
      Friends said I passed my time
The way other men passed water
      But it was my time to spend & live
My time to take back from anybody
      Who tried to waste it
For me   anyone who was left
      To reason out all those things
That don't stand to reason
      The silence on the phone for example
When you answer in the middle of the night
      To find there's no one
No one there   & sure I've spent time

In dives & shit-holes
But in some nice places too even plush
       Hotels on high mountain lakes
& on more than one continent & I've spent
       Weeks in those quaint intolerable inns
Stashed here & there in the countryside
       All around the world
But the place I keep coming back to
       My favorite of them all
Is *this* motel   the one I first came to
       Years ago stumbling down the back
Streets of Winnemucca until I found —
       June's Heavenly Motel & Motor Court
The salvation of a few wayward men
       & at least one wind-blown exhausted boy
So now I'm back again & again who knows
       How long I'll have to stay
Before it seems right once more to leave
       Maybe it's the bar here
That I love most   the chipped ceramic
       Peacocks strutting back & forth
On the treadmill June switches on every
       Night at 11 or so   or maybe
It's the white stucco walls of each unit
       With those roofs of red Spanish tile
The deep emerald doors & window frames
       & the porches all lined with baby
Palm trees   or white roses   or maybe what
       I love more is the old step-up bath
The floors & walls tiled with octagonal pieces
       The size of silver dollars
Each bluer than heaven   bluer than ice
       Even the furniture looks right off

The set of *To Have And Have Not*
        Over-stuffed chairs & rattan tables
Well   I don't know   but when I need to take
        Some time & I have nowhere else to go
I always come back here   here
        Tonight   walking back to my room
With a bucket of ice & a bottle of gin
        I figure I couldn't be doing
Much better   so I turn on the swamp cooler
        Nix the lights & strip down to nothing
In the damp black summer air
        I sit back against the bed's headboard
Holding my glass up to the window
        Where the reflection of June's neon sign
Is flashing on-&-off   on-&-off
        I pour the gin over the snapping ice
Aiming for the lime I know
        Is hunched at the bottom of the glass
& I start to wonder when it was
        That I began to throw in the towel
Before I was asked   as it starts in on me
        Again that awful music of the conscience
& like any man who thinks he carries
        His real life in his mind
Or in his suitcase   I was worthless to
        The woman I married who was still
A child & worthless also to the child
        The daughter I carried
On my shoulders   the rider of a horse
        More wild than either she or I could ever
Have imagined & soon to be more broken
        Sitting alone at nights on the front porch
Watching the lights of the Texaco station
        Go out at 2 A.M. & after that just a

Future of no address no past just a life of
        Marginal destinations
Or once in a while a stop here at June's
        & tonight   on a mirror the size
Of a book I pour out a small mound of crystal
        Methedrine   umber flakes catching
The light outside like shattered quartz
        & with a razor I cut the flakes
To powder then draw the powder with the razor's
        Edge into six thin lines along
The mirror   my own personal *I Ching*
        & with a rolled dollar bill
I finish off each line & with a damp
        Finger clean the silver glossy mirror
Then I lean back against the pillows
        & press my right foot against
The metal rail at the bed's end & I push
        Down & push down as if it were
The pedal of the accelerator in an old truck
        Until my blood laced with methedrine
Lets me feel the way the wind is pouring
        Through the cab's open windows
As the night streaks by   as I speed toward
        A horizon stitched with moonlight
& once again all the broken gauges hanging
        Before me on the darkness
Each as white as the face of a moon
        & all the needles begin to rise slowly
Together   black arms raised at the midnight
        Erect & stiff   each needle pointing
Me on toward some more lasting & final horizon
        One as familiar as the broken white
Line of birds against
                  the black September sky

VI.
LOST MAGIC

Symphonie Tragique

It was the transparence of the air she
Loved, the way the simple wings of dragonflies
Along the riverbank played out the native

Rainbows of the sun. She was the curious,
The restless one, the one who'd leave them all
Forever roped to lives & chores, the lot of them,

The whole wax museum she despised, each corpse
Locked into his woolen suit and shoes,
The locally famous & the bored. She'd had it

With the village men & their attentions,
Their leers & lassitudes, their lurid salutations –
So she refused them everything except

Her shoulder, cocked & shrugging, as she turned
To walk away. It was only her father she regretted
Leaving, as she stood on the platform

Of the town station, the two of them surrounded
By the brash violet of the heather in full bloom.
She knew she'd miss the fog of his voice

At night, as he sang to her accompaniment
Those arias he loved, of all the failed lovers...
Her father held her suitcase absently, our little

World slowing in its whirl, the station master
Handing over the ticket as she told no one,
Bashfully, that she was off to be

The yardage girl at the London *Laura Ashley*.

* * *

It was the transcendence of despair she
Loved, the way black set off her violet eyes,
The carmined glyph of her lips forming

An extravagant sneer as the music
Of the nightclub pounded up through the chairs,
Her body taking each pulse full force,

Driving her through the crowd, wave after wave
Of histrionic zombies, phosphorescent
With sweat, the scent of sex on their breaths,

Driving her toward the stairway of the ladies'
Loo, where she sat before the once shattered & now
Re-glued mirror of the vanity, waiting for night

& her head to clear; then, before her,
The very emblem of that past she'd overheard,
Recognized, the stark melody yet to come —

Assembling like any symphony of air,
Those odd, metallic notes of some familiar song,
Chimes of moonlight along crystal spheres:

& the image of a young girl playing
For her father every piece she's ever known,
The frayed pages of music rising like wings

As he begins to sing in his shadowy baritone,
& the girl fades, not lost, reflected
In the opaque translucence of those polished keys...

By the piano's black, shimmering lake of mirrors.

* * *

It was not the soul but its easy transience
She loved, slowly baring it to him,
First in her letters, then in calls, detailing

The gallery of masks all evil chooses from,
Each carved eyelid vivid in its stare;
At last, he'd come to take her home.

Yet isn't it a daughter's last prerogative
To disagree, to chart a new world without
The blunt lips and the tedious tethers of a man —

Father, lover, son — or anyone at all?
He listened as good fathers do, still quietly
Believing he'd bring her to her senses,

Recalling simply the old riot
Of heather in its April bloom, its violet
Smear along the hillside, its fragrance drifting

Through the open windows of their sitting room.
Still, she was startled when he said so flatly
Within the year he would be dead, or dying,

131

& certainly the idea seemed something
He could more easily bear if she were there;
It was a silence & an end, she knew —

As she knew that one night soon she'd play
For him the endless score of his favorite
And expansively bloody song, the unraveling

Climax of an opera where the lines of time
Slowly braiding schemes and characters
Draw all into their final noose of circumstance,

& he'd sing to her that simple story
Of the terror and pitch of love, of death knowing
Far more than the living should know.

Christmas in Taos

The tree was the tallest spruce
Still standing at the edge of the meadow
Just down the road from the trailer;

He'd dragged it back and set it up
In the metal stand, leaving just enough room
Between the tip of the spruce and the ceiling

For the foil star. She'd baked a few dough
Ornaments — a toy soldier, a rocking horse, tiny
Iced trees. She couldn't look at him

As she hung the limbs with the angel hair
Her mother had given her; she hated him too much
For their threadbare furniture, the junked cars,

The pools of mud with their drawbridge of random
Planks zig zagging from their mailbox to the door.
She hated him for the night that he'd said, No

They couldn't afford to go to the movies, and she
Hated him for the way she wanted him: helplessly, nightly,
Even as she hated the way

He touched her, slowly drawing his hand
Along her ribs and down her thighs all the way until
His thumb and forefinger circled one ankle. Though she

Loved the way the plaid of his shirts wore
To a smooth shine across his shoulders; she loved too
All the things he did for her by hand — a matchbox

He'd made into a car, a doll from scraps of silk.
When she'd finished draping the angel hair, she
Called in her mother to approve. Her mother wrapped

Her arms around the man's waist, the two of them
Together praising her subtle and artistic eye.
Later, her mother dozing on the worn sofa, quietly

They put the few presents under the low boughs.
There was a gift for her wrapped in blue paper; of
Course, she knew what it was. It was the wooden horse

She'd seen him carving the night she snuck out
To the shed, pulling herself up to the high window.
She'd watched for a while as he glued together

The horse's elaborate parts. She'd watched how carefully
He sculpted the flowing blond mane, rippling in long
Waves off the horse's neck and along its back.

And she knew as they knelt beside each other
This horse meant that now they would never be apart;
This was the horse that they would always ride together! —

This was the horse that she rode into the dark.

A Distant Tune

(in memory of Robinson Jeffers)

Where the beach ran out
By the mouth of the narrow river emptying
Into the sea, where the young otters
Basked on the porous, sun-licked rocks,
Where the scrub pine and oat grass whisked
The streaked bellies of birds,
Where the collateral tides measured their worth
At evening and at dawn, where the single tower
Rose like a stone finger toward no God,
The man staring out
At the collapsing sea pulled to his lips
The tarnished flute he'd bought at a pawn shop
In San Francisco and began to play a half-remembered
Melody from Shubert or Mozart or instead that song
He thinks of when he thinks of her
Stepping out onto the stage of the Opera House
As the lights dimmed all around until she
Was left touched by only the single oyster-colored blade
As her voice entered the air
And filled the summer evening, which that evening
Seemed to pulse as quickly as the weary falcon's heart.

A Fortunate Man

Late news and solitude,
A little wine still left in the glass

And the black moon rising. Simple enough
But not enough. He put on his coat

And walked out into the night, hands shoved
Into his coat pockets, a scarf knotted at his neck,

The crust of fever still lining his eyes.
He sat at the counter of the diner, his coffee

Steaming. In the mirror facing him,
Behind the waitress, he could see the blood-red

Graffiti on the opposite wall — the wall
Running along the row of booths behind,

Broken only by a few porthole windows —
Scarlet characters, carmined hieroglyphs,

Spreading confessions. It was
A silver MG pulling up, a low-slung

'A' model splotched with rust slowing,
Outside, at the curb. She just sat there,

The engine running and the radio playing;
She just sat there staring at his back

Through the glass of the door
While he watched her in the long mirror.

He put down some change and turned
From the counter, and as he stood he felt

The collapse of the air all around him,
The shimmering of the very light

He stood within, and sweat
Pearled along the ridge above his lips.

Outside the diner, he swayed a moment,
Leaning against the silver fender;

Then he got in. As they stopped for a light
He turned to face the reflection rippling

Along the shop window beside him; it was
A bakery, rows and rows of eclairs

And regal napoleans, a silver car, a woman,
Her black-gloved hands on the wheel,

And a man whose simple travels
Would be ending, soon,

Perhaps in a room in his daughter's house
Above the bay, where the feather ferns drifted

Quietly outside the windows and pepper trees
Drooped along the drive, where he could

Look down and see each morning the silver MG
Still freckled with dew, knowing nothing, knowing

Only the relief that all of the Books of Praise
Promise a fortunate man.

Disquiet Fortunes

Who knows why the night fails?—
Finally, even the parliamentary doves
Succumb to fortunes riven by
The scavenging rain. Any news of love
Erupts in the body suddenly
& mysteriously, to keep its pain
Vital, viscous, & new. Those
Days, I lived in the Algerian quarter
Of the Fifth, on the Rue Dulay. Each
Evening, the old baker on the corner
Stepped out & shook his canvas apron
Until the streets filled with pillows
Of swirling flour. A white dusk falling
As all of the cafés began to fill, as I sat
In the tiny park just below Celestine's
Room — her paints, her cats, torn
Rolls of canvas everywhere — waiting, as
She'd pace through the night, smoking
Or crying or cutting lines of heroin. We
Were both too solitary to know
What to do with each other, let alone
How to come in from that milky & eternal
Night. She said, Change is like blame —
A lost, & unlikely forgiveness. Never the rain
& its cover of darkness, never those holy
Predicates of sin. Please, she said, just
This once *become* me. Hold me. We'd walk
To the park & its dying stand of pines; we'd
Touch the white, chalked initials covering
The blackened char of the cemetery gate —
We felt fictive & poised, though not yet

138

Desolate...not weak. The ritual of the day itself
Became crystal & twisted by the blue of dawn.
The single long window of her bedroom
Webbed by the veins of frost
Until the sun slid by. One morning
I recognized all was lost: the scent of her hair
Uncoiling as she walked in from the bath,
The taste of her skin familiar as swollen
Figs slowly melting on the tongue. Still,
What other choices does a simple life
Allow?— Just these brilliant stages of decline
Along the breath. The curtain closing
On a silent theater, the theater itself empty
Of everyone but us. That giddy
& ridiculously bold sexual
Glare ricocheting off our bodies & into
Some indiscreet smoke of day, until an evening
Falls like the one now gathering in this café,
A kind of familiar party
Of continuance. I know those odd
Distractions of the weather might seem
Shop-worn to you, & tawdry, so forgive me;
Yet don't forget it's easy to be unfair. It's
Enough to drive any man to several
Serious espressos after waking to
An emptiness
That tastes like Celestine's body, & missing
That rush of hair across the pillow as,
Slowly, I rise from the grotto of dream. You
Know, it started only moments ago, that wild
Trilling of drops along the filthy skylight
Just above the bed. She'd always wanted
To make the rain something personal — not

That anonymous sentence above, as the wind
Whipped the black summer trees. She'd
Touch my shoulders in the dark,
Quietly dragging
The tips of her fingers, the spider of
Her hand along my spine — & as I'd turn
To look up at her, I'd see the silence of
My gaze, reflected, the way a lake
Grows finally to regard
The newly restless & ever-deepening
Sky. Then she'd ask again that question
She asked each morning until
The end. Who knows why? I stayed there
Almost forever. Never doubting the night fails.

Cavalacanti's Dream: World's End

I walked the curving, mercury stairway
    Spiraling far beyond the moon
        In its languid way never meant

For men. There I saw how we'd be left
    Only Mary's stained & ancient veils, unfolding
        Before us slowly as sails

On our way to the rendezvous beneath the tower
    Where black clouds rippled closely
        As the hour. Those soft, wooden slats

Of the drawbridge rails...still torn
    Delicately as flesh by random nails; the sky
        Itself printed with God's seal, that

Festering white eye, mute zero ablaze with fire,
    Wheeling out the fate of the faithful as they kneel...
        A world lost until some final future

Sin, when the heart stands able to begin again.

Mirror

Once I believed
We would live inside the pearl forever,

Its opacity the single mirror in which
We slept. How could I understand

That I was not the reason for your unhappiness,
When I wanted to be everything to you?

Aspects of Solange

I.

Where are the sky's ambassadors tonight?

Weeping no doubt yes I have no doubt
They are most certainly weeping
By the smoky wine-colored fire

Now the long black rake of the rain has arrived

II.

So she praised the pale violet riders
Passing over the broken heath
She praised the passage of black islands
Rising along her body & beyond the ravel of lips

She praised the opulent spray of the waves
& the smokey blush of recognition as that satin
Of evening light wrapped her naked shoulders
She praised her own fine scent & its ghostliness

Weaving together the lesions of night

III.

The old villa reflected the silver light of ancient stones
Along every stairway
                    Those endless ascents & pitches of terrible
Precipice where below her father's vineyards stretched
For miles to the mountains

& out of the silence of the moment Solange's sister
Stepped from a doorway holding her coat in one hand saying
Abruptly

Don't you think it's time we were going?

IV.

The days grew older but quietly

Against the driver's side window of the car
Red-&-gold maple leaves pressed like the hands of supplicants

As the white stumps of fence posts picked off the miles
Toward a horizon sharp & scoured as a burnished bowl —

Sun-lit & brittle; almost aflame...

V.

The fountain in the hospital courtyard
Touched the pursed lips of the wind
The fallen palm fronds slowly littered
The cobbled stones of the path
Leading along the tall white & pulsing walls

No more interior fortunes at work
This evening as she steps a bit closer
To the mirror of the room's ancient vanity
Her face skeletal in the radium moon of the clock

& she fans brushstrokes of rouge along each cheekbone

As the quiet incline of her breath disperses like a mist
The cautionary light gathering slowly
Toward her eclipse

VI.

How hard then to be home
Even the gnarled sheep-like shrubs

Fell to their knees along the heath
Beneath the sweep of the butterscotch wind

The scent of damp wool hung in the air
With the scent of the cedar slats

He'd thrown onto the fire the night before
Just as she'd called to him from the bed

Piled high with animal skins & ancient blankets
Her arms so thin & bare chiming

With silver bracelets collapsing together
As she lifted her hands to his face & the musk

Seeping in at the dark edges of the window
Unrolled like a calendar of those future nights

He would awaken simply naked & alone
In the absent shine of her body

VII.

— & so she left them all behind
Weeping no doubt yes I have no doubt
They were most certainly weeping
As the carver's chisel scored the stone

& then the sky rang bright as bone

Lost Magic

Photographs: some in the style of Lana Turner
(My father later said, "No, more Merle Oberon"),
Head tossed slightly back, auburn curls lightly
Falling on her shoulders. I loved each of them,
Those glamorous shots quietly reflecting
The dreams of every Forties movie, & her own.
Still, there's another photo that's
Stayed with me in a way that others couldn't,
Though even now I can't explain it, really.
My mother, barely more than a teenager,
Is standing beside a young man dressed up
As a magician — jaunty top hat, white gloves,
Even a phony mustache balancing dangerously
On his thin, hairless top lip, being
No less a kid than she. Yet, there they are,
This magic act: my mother in a mildly risqué
But elegant white dress serving as the assistant,
Waiting to step into that black mock coffin —
Smiling as the saw divides her from herself,
However briefly. As a boy, I could never
Pry those secrets from her, not a single one;
She'd taken an oath, she said, & a magician
& even a magician's assistant would never
Go back on their word. And so, for me, trust
Seemed forever linked to magic, every
Secret worth knowing held behind the eyelashes
Of that young girl in the photograph
Performing "Ancient Egyptian Mysteries"
& the "Secrets of the Fakirs!" to sick kids
At the Children's Hospital, to the stony-faced
Old men wheezing at the Elks Club. Tonight,

Remembering my own son at five, maybe six,
Practicing over & over the magic cups
& ball trick, astonishing even himself with every
Successful sleight of hand, I think I sense the pulse
Of pleasures once held close to the breast,
Or else, simply, that worldly measure of their loss.

Elegy

It's true such reckless grace should never die,
Just as it's true that death itself is meaningless
To the silver gulls riding the summer sky.

Out of the dust of ancient motorcycle lies,
Beyond the sinless vaudeville one should not confess,
It's true, such a reckless grace should never die

Into some hope that's lifted like an angel's sigh —
Like that black ace hidden in the parrot's vest
As it flies beside the riders of the sky.

So let me wear my anger for a while, my
Last good suit, though I'd feel much better dressed
It's true, wearing your old reckless grace. "Never die,"

You once said to me, "Or else, try to surprise
The gods when they're busy fucking; that's more or less
My idea: to go off low-riding a bloody summer sky."

Un coup de des... les jeux sont faits. I still despise
The empty shadow this last, single die has cast
Along those silver wings lighting the summer sky.
My friend, such reckless grace should never die.

My Grandfather's Cap

There are so few photographs of him,
Peter Fries, my mother's quiet
Father, baker and bar owner, patriarch
Of silence and five daughters, one son,
And a past distinguished, I discover,
Late one night rummaging haphazardly
Through an old bureau drawer,
By a secret life in baseball. Along
The huge arm
Of the old horsehair sofa,
I lay three snapshots: two of Pete
Off fishing with some pals
High in the Sierras; and the last,
His team photo, taken some early
Summer evening, before the season's
Last minor league game....
He's stretched out, leaning on one elbow,
Surrounded by his boyish teammates,
Himself, even more boyish,
His jersey scripted with the sponsor's
Name, *Bittels*, and his soft felt cap —
The one I remember hooked
On the metal barb jutting off the coat rack
Just inside the door, the one
With the ghost of a "B" along its crown,
Signifying my entire childhood —
Pulled down over one eye,
Just like a displaced Bowery Boy.
In that first fishing shot, he's wearing
A straw hat and looking for all the world,
I'm afraid, quite frighteningly

Like Maurice Chevalier...
Sitting on a huge fallen log
Between two friends, squinting
Into the diamond of the camera lens
In the high mountain sunlight at the lake's
Edge. In the second, he's squatting
Indian style on the flat
Ancient wood of an anonymous pier,
His five jaunty buddies hamming it up
With rods and buckets, but not
A single caught fish anywhere in sight!
It's this one I keep holding up
To the glare of the crook-necked lamp,
Trying to make out in the faded sepia
Of this muddy print
The crumpled cap he's wearing,
Pulled down over the same narrow slit
Of an eye, half closed, half winking,
A cap suspiciously familiar
Even though it's twenty years later —
His old baseball cap, its felt worn
To an oily shine, a shine like those scales
Strewn along the planks at his feet,
Pale stars weighing
Almost nothing in the air and light,
Weighing less, even, than an early
Summer evening settling
Around a boy in a wool jersey with a life
As yet unreckoned, the crowd noise
Slowly rising as the crack of the bat
Lifts a tiny white balloon
Into the sky, as he runs, breathless, alone,
Stretching as far as his body will allow

Into my present, our lines striking
The water of the sky, both of us reaching
For those stilled, carefully stitched
Seams of this yet distant, yet pale, future
And now forever-rising moon.

VII.
IN THE PINES

Lavender Disaster

It was in the old days in Atlantic City
& as the icy rain began to clear the boardwalks

Of even the most desolate stragglers

I pulled my ultra-cool thrift store fedora
Down low over my eyes & just kept on walking

& as I passed an old storefront painted up

Like a fortuneteller's bazaar its ancient bricks
Covered in narrow stripes of orange and lavender

As if it were a gypsy's rippling tent

The old woman inside said softly to me the words
Come try & nothing else but after a few steps

I turned & went back & stepped out of the rain

To face her across the small round table
Where she sat shuffling a bent pack of tarot cards

Sit down she said & of course I did just that

& as she laid the cards out slowly before her
She quietly rocked a little in her chair

Then told me the story of the future I might hold

& as she spoke the room filled with a light
As thick as the mist outside & softly lavender

As softly lavender as an electric summer sunset

Down at the beach with maybe Stella or even Renata
& the gypsy's eyes closed & my own eyes too

And she said *You will sit in the throne of Heaven*

& die into the open arms of your Lord
Well that's really nice I thought

All this death shit & not a word about sex or money

But I couldn't open my eyelids for a second
& when I did the mist had cleared although a faint

Scent remained of my grandmother's lavender sachet

& the gypsy's hand was out so I slapped down a five
Then got out before she told me something else

I didn't want to know but I was worse than chilly now

A little bent out of shape & leery of the way
The night was coming down so black along the streets

I just knew I couldn't go on to work that night

So I turned back & started heading home thinking
How Stella would be pissed I'd spent that five spot

On the gypsy not to mention I'd be back

Early with no money from the shift I couldn't do
But maybe we'd go out to the movies

We hadn't done that since I'd been made a night clerk

That would make her happy I thought the movies
& then a drink at Jake's to make up for the fact

We'd be broke again next week for sure

& as I opened the door to our apartment
I swear I could smell the scent of lavender

& that same mist began rolling through the living room

& I could hear them then in the back bedroom
Making those little fucking sounds so fucking softly

So fucking tenderly it made me want to scream

But I just walked through the kitchen & grabbed
The ice pick off the counter where Stella'd

Left it after chipping ice flakes for their drinks

& as I came to the open bedroom door
I stood there for a second but

They didn't notice me her legs fiercely bicycling

The air & he was jack-hammering away at her
So I just stepped up beside the bed & punctuated

This happy dream with a few decisive holes

To let the lavender air out of the moment
& I'm not kidding as I watched the two of them

Stretched out silently across the damp mattress

I could actually see the mist clearing again
& again I could finally breathe a little

So none of the rest of this really matters

& you reading this matter least of all
Because I am the one man who knows my simple

Future & all of the rest of you must live in the pain

Of not knowing of not believing what comes
Will be finally not so different from my own

Wild glory as I come to sit at last upon

My own Lordly throne so carefully hewn
Of precious woods & polished by the sweat of men

Who before me have mistakenly believed only

They were worthy of this journey I welcome
As I am fitted with those perfect leather straps

A helmet wired to the future & charged by the grace

Of God & the Governor to carry me into that Heaven
I was promised one distant lavender

Night

The Widow of Peter the Great

I.

I suppose this is the day,
My darling, to tell you the whole
Long story of
My sadness; after all, this
Is something a daughter should
At last be told, and it is the mother,
Surely, who should tell. You have
Heard — already —
That I was a beautiful girl,
Of the many men who courted me
From the day that I turned twelve,
& how my stern father simply
Laughed them all away. You
Have heard
From your grandmother
That tiresome story of the prince
Who bored me utterly to sleep
At the Winter Palace's Summer Ball —
But you have not heard why,
The year I turned seventeen, in every
Village across the Ukraine, they
Began to call me "The Widow"
After the night my father took out
His antique hunting rifle from its
Elaborately tooled leather case...
No, I have never told you this...
How it was my very own father
Who went out & shot Peter the Great.

II.

Seventeen is too young
For any woman to become a widow,
& for some time I confess
I tried simply to pretend
The world still turned methodically
From night to day, that Peter
The Great had been nothing to me,
Only the dearest friend
Any woman might ask for. Yet
The truth of the matter
Is something I have lived with
& told no one until you, my darling
Daughter, on this this day. I know
Too it is impossible
To lay blame at the feet of my father,
Who was, of course, a remarkable man.
And what a life we had, travelling
Across the whole of Europe & Russia
With the finest circuses in the world!

*   *   *

Father's performing bears were always
The featured attraction. And how
Magnificent he would look
As he stepped into the spotlight,
His brushed black tails
Shimmering like satin fur as the silver
Rod in his hand rose & each
Dazzling bear would
Begin to dance slowly into the center

Of the ring. He'd lead them through
The gentle humorous tricks:
The silly bicycle riding,
The walking on huge golden spheres
While rolling little white rings
Off their snouts & high into the air!
But it was the Pyramid of Seven Bears
That was unlike anything
The world knew. At
The base, the four steady
Older rocks, all Siberians; then,
Balanced sidewise
On their backs, two younger Black bears,
Bristling & nervous, wildly lovely;
At the top, always the single
Sensational Siberian silver giant
My father had trained so carefully
& especially for this act —
His prize bear, standing slowly upright,
Each of its huge hind paws squared
On the heads of the two somewhat
Unhappy Black bears below! What a sight
It was, & what constant applause! My
Father would hold them
In this pyramid
For no more than a few seconds,
But it seemed to the rapt audience
Like the passage of several days,
& with the flick of my father's
Long silver rod
The prize Siberian on top — suddenly
& to the astonishment of the crowd —
Would back-flip from that terrible

Height into the net
My two brothers & I had moved silently
Alongside the pyramid while
The audience had reached its roaring peak
Of admiration! Of course
It never failed to bring even
The most lackadaisical matinee crowd
To its feet howling. So, naturally, my
Father & our bears were in great demand.
Yet I should confess that
Even we never expected that elegant,
Wax-sealed command invitation
To come immediately to St. Petersburg —
With a few of our most select
& carefully chosen circus friends — to perform
For the Czar himself. My mother nearly
Fainted from the excitement; my brothers
Began giggling breathlessly
Repeating to me the stories of the Czar's
Legendary sexual prowess. My father
Slapped each of them & went out
Proudly to his friends
To arrange for the caravan of wagons
That would take us to the Czar & the dawn
That would forever after mark my life.

III.

We set up in a small, gorgeous
Clearing in that famous
Park at the edge of St. Petersburg;
The wagons & cages were all arranged
In precise half-moons

Cupping each other like the bodies of
Lovers. One morning,
As we led all of the bears once again
Through their familiar routines,
We heard in the distance the roll
Of rising thunder as the Czar's
Horsemen appeared
Completely out of nowhere,
Like the shadows of storm clouds
Moving through the trees; & then,
His special guard in their
Billowing scarlet uniforms & fur caps
Lit up the road leading to our camp.
Slowly, majestically, an elaborate carriage
Came into view, its wood polished
The orange of a pumpkin. As it
Stopped in the center of the clearing,
The swirling dust still
Shifting & falling in its steady currents,
The Czar himself stepped out of its door!
He was so astonishingly tall —
The top of my head came just level
With his wide silver belt — and cruelly
Handsome. The Czar & my serious father
Walked slowly around the carriage,
Talking quietly & intently;
Then my father drew himself up like
The host of some
Miraculous party, & happily led
The Czar from wagon to wagon,
as he graciously
& proudly introduced each of the acts
He'd brought with us for the Czar's pleasure:

First, the twin Spanish albino
Trapeze artists (brother & sister, secret
Lovers too); then the twelve French midget
Tumblers, a constantly moving human
Kaleidoscope; the beautiful painted lady
My father had once
Surprised in her calm bath one evening,
As she stood naked, shaving
The complicated continents of her legs.
And perhaps that day too she'd been
Called out from her bath, because
She stood there shivering in the spring
Winds, as if all the colors of her
Paint had stolen the heat from her body.
The Czar, staring a moment
At her elaborately painted & quivering
Flesh, stepped forward & opened his enormous
Black coat, then pulled it slowly from his own
Shoulders & draped it lightly across hers!
It was the single most gallant thing
I had ever seen; she stood there, the coat
So huge it lay
Gathered in folds & ripples
Like black waves at her feet. The Czar
Bent down to kiss her on the top
Of her head. I was amazed, as he could not
Have known what I knew: that she
Considered it the most sacred & sensual
Place on her body, the one place
She had chosen to leave bare of any paint.
And when he stepped back & she looked

Up at him, it was as if the sweet petals
Of her body had slowly unfolded. Then, quite
Tactfully, my father suggested that we go on,
& at last we came to the bears' famous quarters.

*   *   *

My father had refused to call them "cages"
& he'd insisted that old but elegant
Oriental rugs be laid out along the cold
Floors, that huge sculptural logs be rolled in,
& that boulders be stacked around
The wide flat basins of water where our bears
Bathed & drank. There we all stood,
At last, in those lightly-barred
Apartments suitable for almost anyone,
& my father proudly introduced one
By one each of his amazing bears!—
Natasha, Sergei, Anton, Fortunato,
Anna, and Feydor. Then he led
The Czar to his prize bear, its coat
Gleaming like a silver aurora borealis,
Seventeen feet on his hind legs; & that
Day he rose to his full height —
As slowly & majestically as a prince —
Meeting another prince —
The very moment
He saw us approaching with the Czar.
He was, with no doubt, the single
Most beautiful creature in the world.
This is what the Czar said to my proud
Father, & which I too believed. "This one,"
My father said shyly, " I have taken

165

The liberty of naming after you..." And
The Czar smiled broadly, then began
Laughing as he stared up
At his own towering namesake, his own
Unnatural mirror. Silent a moment, the Czar
Said solemnly, "I've always heard you were
A bit *larger* than life, my dear Peter!"
And with that the Czar and all of his special
Guard erupted in laughter, while Peter
The Great, still standing on
His hind legs, began swaying his huge head
Slowly back and forth. The Czar unhooked
His thick silver belt from his tunic;
He lifted it up so we
Could see it blazing in the sunlight. Then
He signaled my father to open the door
To Peter the Great's apartment. My
Father hesitated for a moment,
& then nodded for me to hand him the long
Skeleton key I wore on a red ribbon
Around my neck, a most
Sacred trust. As the door swung open
The Czar stepped into the cage alone, so
Fearlessly, & the man who had
Never looked up
To anyone stood there gazing clearly
Up into the eyes of the enormous bear, who,
Almost mystically hypnotized, began
To slowly lower his head
Until the Czar
Could drape the silver belt around
Peter the Great's shoulders, hooking it
Carefully like some kingly necklace. As

The Czar stepped back, Peter
Rose again to his full height & roared
So loudly the Czar's guards
Drew their revolvers,
But the Czar held up one hand, & touching
Peter the Great's huge paw, said only,
"Goodbye, my secret soul...."
Stepping out of Peter's quarters, the Czar
Winked at me, "Take good care of *this*
Peter the Great; who knows, one day
Perhaps *he'll* be Czar!" And he
Began laughing as he walked slowly
To his waiting carriage. With my own father!

* * *

I felt dizzy, breathless;
As I turned to look back at Peter's cage;
I saw that he had extended his huge
Left paw to me, a paw as wide as a café table,
& he was beckoning me in. I suppose
It was that day
I began to love him, really,
Seeing how truly royal he was, seeing how
Even the Czar respected him. I'd spend
All of my spare time with Peter,
Training him I told my father; & of course
It was in those days
I helped Peter the Great discover
What it meant to be truly human, just as Peter
Helped me to learn at last what it meant
To feel part of the whole natural
Weather of the world, part

Of the pulse that carries the rare tenderness
Of the world along its soft & rivery ways.

IV.

And when at last, one night,
My father came out simply to check
The grounds for prowlers & to see that every
Bear was sleeping & secure, when at last
He pulled back the curtain at the front
Of Peter the Great's cage, of course
He could see me, naked & curled
Like a maidenhair fern on Peter's warm back
Like a baby about to have her picture painted
On the studio rug. My father's
Bellow awakened us both, & as I snatched up
My clothes, I threw open the door, trying
To lead Peter out into the grounds,
Away from my father— but Peter
Lept to the top of those logs he had scarred
& sculpted with his claws, mirrored by the basin
Of the water, rocking above the landscape
Of the oriental rugs we'd laid out for him;
Then he reached to the Czar's
Silver belt & hung it like a heavy noose
Around his own neck. He rose roaring
To his hind legs, swaying like a monk in prayer —
I could see my father coming back, the rifle
Shaking in his hands. I screamed at my father
& swore at him, & he stopped dead
In his tracks,
No more than thirty feet away from us;
He took aim at Peter the Great

& Peter's own enormous eyes closed briefly
As he swayed & swayed, then in an instant
As they blazed open & he stepped
To charge, my father pulled the trigger
& one of those beautiful black eyes
Exploded — I howled & howled, until
The rifle fired again & a swirling crowd of
Wailing midgets gathered, pulling
Me back, all hugging me as I collapsed
Onto the ground. Crying, crying, crying....

*   *   *

And so you see my daughter, why
Today, the day of your own father's death,
Why all of the people from my old
Village in Ukraine came to call me
Unlucky, so unlucky—a widow twice now
Before I'm forty. And finally you know
Why for all these years
I have loved to wear this fat silver belt
Around my simple ashen tunics, so
Long it could circle my waist twice,
So wide I could pull it across my bare breasts
Like some outlaw's prized bandolier.
And yes, in that precious picture
I keep on the mantle, the very one
Of you as a baby at only three months,
White as a slug on the dark silver fur, yes,
That flat pile of tanned hide is all
That remains of the hatred I taste for my father;
All that remains of the girl who danced for a bear;
All that remains of that luminous body praised by a Czar.

In the Pines

Vertical spindles of shadow, the black
Firs & violet pines surround
This open meadow broken
Only by a pond
Illuminated like an old Bible
With flakes of gold leaf; & beside
The pond, a hunter's decrepit shack
I've claimed, its split planks
Chinked with plaster & old rags. Just
Today, I've spent
The morning poking out a bird's nest
Lodged in the crooked brick chimney
Pointing up
Through the roof like a single
Broken finger... Here, the only
Accusing voices are those
Of the branches snapping & smoking
In the stove, of the gray squirrels chasing
The one albino out of their trees
To, I imagine,
Some ghetto of oak or maple
reserved for him; & look, his tail
Is as erect as a white feather
Pen, a plume dipped into its tiny, snowy
Inkwell, the spine of the tail quivering
As the fronds of hair
Are blown by a rising breeze. Here,
I can do as I wish; that is, nothing.
I was told the words
I could use most tactfully
With relatives & friends included, *"recovery"*

& *"recuperation,"* or even, *"a simple rest,"*
The doctor said while handing my last
Check to his indifferent nurse.
Fuck them all, I thought,
I'm never coming back. Besides, they have
No way of knowing
I have a "friend" now, though
She is beyond — & I mean this quite
Literally — any description they might
Understand. I first heard her singing
One evening at dusk
As I began to boil the water
For my coffee. I was sure it was a song
I knew though couldn't place, & the singer's
Voice was more lovely than any
I could remember...When I stepped out
Into the clearing, walking a few yards
Along the muddy lip of the pond,
I could see her sitting
High in the branches of a tall, nearby pine;
Slowly, her wings — blond wings the breadth
Of a man's body — began to work
So beautifully & rhythmically to the song
She sang
            that she rose
Out of the pines, circling above the cabin
& the pond, circling lower, lower
Until I could see she had a woman's face,
The whole shining head of a woman...
Long wheat-colored hair
Floating back over her arced wings;
& her face just wasn't any woman's face,
It was a face even more delicate & lovely

Than her song. Her body was the body
Of a condor: just as powerful, graceful, sleek...
& though I knew her name
From childhood books, from my father's
Leather-bound *Bullfinch*, I knew
That name was wrong, absolutely wrong, so
Very absurd & wrong. She
Was so much more like an angel, if more
Beautiful than any I could have dreamed;
There was no question: *like an angel.*
For three days,
She came each evening to the pond
& sang for me; then, on the fourth night,
She disappeared... Thank God that now,
As dusk has just began to fall, I can
See that she's returned to sit
In the stiff, umber limbs of the pine
At the clearing's edge, a pine I watched
Shiver & sway, but never fall, as lightning
Touched it, in the summer's first
Electric storm. In these days
That she's been gone, her song's grown
So much sadder; yet
                    I know it now by heart,
Its endless double stairways, its empty
Circular courts. This evening,
I'll call her down to the fallen oak by
The pond, coaxing her to rest in its low branches
While I stroke her hair, running my hands
From the narrow slope
Of her shoulders down along her delicate
Spine, over the long white-&-gold feathers
Falling limply from the small of

Her back. I'll lift those feathers, letting
Them spread across my chest like the damp fan
Of an emperor's courtesan, the tips
Of the long feathers
Cutting my neck like fine razors
As I unbuckle my pants & pull myself
Into her, her talons gripping
The long scarred branches of the oak
& with each thrust of my body —
Her body arching back into mine...
At last, I know
Our motion together is more than angel
& man, bird & man, world & man...
Her wings begin unfolding beneath me
As I lean forward, my mouth closing on
The fine gold down swirling
At the nape of her neck —
We rise slowly out of the oak, the long
Strokes of her wings forcing our bodies
To lock tightly together; I will not
Let myself look back
Until I know we're far above the needles of
The pines, far above the high range marking
The horizon. Yet, when I do look,
I can see the smoke of my
Dinner fire still rising from the bent
Brick finger; the cabin roof, with its random
Squares of tar & plastic, looks so lovely,
Like a child's patchwork quilt thrown casually
Over the quiet, suddenly still crib... Then,
She begins to sing again, very
Softly at first;
As we climb, I can see

               the rocks below
Are topped by tiny caps of snow, the air
Tasting of minerals, of rain...
& I know soon now
She'll tire of my weight, tire of
Lifting any man this near the empty heavens;
& I know my lungs in this clarity of air
Will last no longer than
Her song. Though I hardly care, though
I foresaw it all, still,
I know as well as she knows — in stories
Of this kind — when what comes
Has come finally to its end, which of us
Must fall...